THE GERMAN IDEOLOGY

Karl Marx
and
Frederick Engels

THE GERMAN IDEOLOGY
Part One

with selections from Parts Two and Three, together with Marx's
"Introduction to a Critique of Political Economy"

Edited
and with Introduction by
C. J. ARTHUR

INTERNATIONAL PUBLISHERS
NEW YORK

PUBLISHER'S NOTE: References in the text to *The German Ideology,* London, 1965, are to the complete work, published simultaneously by Lawrence & Wishart, London, and Progress Publishers, Moscow. (*The German Ideology, Parts I and III*, edited with an introduction by R. Pascal, was published by International Publishers, New York, 1947, with the eighth reprint appearing in 1969.) The page references in the present book to Karl Marx, *The Economic and Philosophic Manuscripts of 1844* are to the Lawrence & Wishart and Progress Publishers edition of 1959; another edition of this work, edited with an introduction by Dirk J. Struik, was published by International Publishers, 1964.

 209

Library of Congress Catalog Card Number: 71-148517
SBN (cloth) 7178-0301-5; (paperback) 7178-0302-3
Printed in the United States of America

CONTENTS

SUPPLEMENTARY TEXTS

EDITOR'S PREFACE

The Complete Edition of Marx and Engels' early work, *The German Ideology*, comprises more than 700 pages. The bulk of it consists of detailed line by line polemics against the writings of some of their contemporaries. This is likely to be of interest only to scholars. However, in the first part of the work, ostensibly concerned with Feuerbach, the authors work quite differently. What they do is to set out at length their own views, in so doing providing one of their earliest accounts of materialism, revolution, and communism—as trenchant and exciting as anything they ever wrote, including the *Manifesto*. Hence the usefulness of the present abridgement, based on this material.

The bulk of *The German Ideology* was written between September 1845 and the summer of 1846. By that time the greater part of the first volume had been written—namely the chapters devoted to the criticism of the views of Bauer and Stirner—and the second volume, on "True" Socialism, for the most part also. The authors continued to work on the first section of Volume 1 (the criticism of Ludwig Feuerbach's views) during the second half of 1846, but did not complete it.

In May 1846 the major part of the manuscript of Volume 1 was sent from Brussels to Joseph Weydemeyer in Westphalia. Weydemeyer was to make arrangements for the publication of the book with the financial support that had been promised by two local businessmen, the "true" socialists Julius Meyer and Rudolph Rempel. But after the bulk of the manuscript of Volume 2 had arrived in Westphalia, Meyer and Rempel informed Marx that they were unwilling to finance the publication of *The German Ideology*. In 1846–47 Marx and Engels made repeated attempts to find a publisher in Germany for their work; their efforts were, however, unsuccessful. This was due partly to difficulties made by the police and partly to the reluctance of the publishers to print the work since their sympathies were on the side of the representatives of the trends attacked by Marx and Engels.

Marx remarked later that they then abandoned the MS. to "the gnawing criticism of the mice". This turned out to be literally true, and affected passages have been reconstructed by the editors of the Complete Edition, by inserting words, which are enclosed in square brackets.

The extant manuscript of the first chapter "Feuerbach" consists of pages halved lengthwise into two columns, the left filled with most of the text in Engels' script—he wrote more smoothly and quickly than Marx—from joint dictation. The right-hand column has many additions from both authors. It was never completed and unfortunately even the existing material was not revised and turned into a structured whole. Thus the incorporation of the marginalia and the arrangement of the material poses a considerable editorial problem. The editors of the Complete Edition state:

"The headings and the arrangement of the material in the chapter 'Feuerbach' are based on notes by Marx and Engels found in the margins of the manuscript, and on the contents of the chapter."[1]

Such criteria still leave considerable discretion to the editor, as may be seen by comparing with the Complete Edition prepared by the Institute of Marxism-Leninism, Moscow (English trans. 1965), another version of Part One in *Writings of the Young Marx on Philosophy and Society*, edited by L. D. Easton and K. H. Guddat (New York, 1967).

In preparing this popular edition I have tried to ensure that the arrangement of the material is as readable as possible. So that the reader can find his way about in it I have broken up the text by section headings, almost all of which are my own.

Although I am responsible for the arrangement of the material, the translation (very slightly revised) is that of the Complete Edition of 1965; the chapter "Feuerbach" translated by W. Lough, and the remaining parts by C. Dutt and C. P. Magill.

All but two or three paragraphs of Chapter One, "Feuerbach", are presented here.

As previously mentioned, the remaining chapters of *The German Ideology* contain super-polemics against Stirner and others. However, there do exist "oases in the desert" in which Marx and Engels make interesting points, throwing additional light on the topics dealt with in Chapter One. I have selected a number of such passages, and again provided my own headings. In addition, a summary of the omitted parts has been provided in an introductory essay.

Also from this period of Marx's life are the *Theses on Feuerbach*, discovered by Engels amongst Marx's papers, and published by him in a polished version in 1888. Here we present the original version, since Engels' is widely available in anthologies.

[1] *The German Ideology*, Lawrence and Wishart, London, 1965, p. 670.

Another Addendum is an "Introduction" written by Marx in 1857 which deserves to be much more widely known, and is an interesting treatment, some eleven years later than *The German Ideology*, of aspects of materialist method. This "Introduction" is included in the mass of work published as *"Grundrisse"*. It is an incomplete draft of a "general introduction" for the great economic work planned by Marx, the main points of which he already indicates in this introduction. In his further researches Marx changed his original plan several times, and *Critique of Political Economy*, 1859, and *Capital*, were thus created. The introduction was found among Marx's papers in 1902, and was first published in *Neue Zeit* in 1903.

The notes and indexes have been adapted from the Complete Edition of *The German Ideology*. The Index of Names and Authorities also contains notes on the references where appropriate.

EDITOR'S INTRODUCTION

The German Ideology of 1846 is the first recognisably "Marxist" work—although, as the authors themselves state, their earlier publications, essays in the *Deutsch-Französische Jahrbücher* and *The Holy Family*, "pointed the way". Also we now know of the *Economic and Philosophic Manuscripts of 1844* by Marx, in which the German idealists' concept of "Alienation" had been decisively transformed and rooted in the labour process. However, the latter work could still be considered an extension of Feuerbach's humanism.[1] It was not until 1845–1846 that Marx and Engels took their distance from Feuerbach —although he is not criticised in detail in *The German Ideology*. Here is how Engels recalls that period in the *Preface* to his essay on Feuerbach of 1888:

> "Before sending these lines to press I have once again ferreted out and looked over the old manuscript of 1845–46. The section dealing with Feuerbach is not completed. The finished portion consists of an exposition of the materialist conception of history which proves only how incomplete our knowledge of economic history still was at that time. It contains no criticism of Feuerbach's doctrine itself; for the present purpose, therefore, it was unusable. On the other hand, in an old notebook of Marx's I have found the eleven theses on Feuerbach printed here as an appendix. These are notes hurriedly scribbled down for later elaboration, absolutely not intended for publication, but invaluable as the first document in which is deposited the brilliant germ of the new world outlook."[2]

The excitement and exultation of the authors armed with their new world outlook can still be felt almost palpably in the pages of *The German Ideology*, just as it can in the *Manifesto* two years later.

In order to grasp the position that Marx and Engels had reached in 1846 it may be useful to retrace their route, in the course of which such technical terms as "civil society" and "alienation" can be explained.

[1] This view is persuasively argued in D. McLellan, *The Young Hegelians and Karl Marx*, London, 1969.
[2] Marx-Engels *Selected Works*, 1962, Vol. II, p. 359.

Hegel

As is well known, in Hegel's social philosophy the State played a key role. The State is the rule of reason in society, the incarnation of freedom. After Hegel's death his followers began to diverge. The "Left" or "Young" Hegelians, broadly speaking, began to criticise (their favourite word) the existing State by declaring that it was not yet in accordance with its "idea". It must be reformed.

Marx soon began to take a much more radical view. As early as 1843 he had, in effect, arrived at the position that to free the State of its deficiencies would be, in the ultimate, to abolish it.[1]

A key term in this connection, which is also employed in *The German Ideology*, is *civil society*. When Marx and Engels talk about "Bürgerliche Gesellschaft", this term is sometimes inaccurately translated as "bourgeois society". On the one hand it has the meaning of "civilised society", i.e. society with government, laws, etc., as opposed to "natural" or primitive society; and also serves to denote the personal and economic relations of men as opposed to political relations and forms (which distinction can most obviously be made of modern times). It arose and was used in the seventeenth and eighteenth centuries amongst bourgeois theoreticians as a tool in their theoretical attack on political forms which prevented the free accumulation of private property.

In Hegel's philosophy *civil society* has a prominent role as that sphere in which man is constituted as a separate individual. His interests are civil and economic, not political. He does not feel himself a participant in public affairs, but views the State as an external necessity of which he has to take account. His particular interests appear as distinct from, and opposed to, the general interests represented by the State. However, the possibility of a conciliation of this conflict is based on the fact that men are creatures of reason; they have a universal side and so can accept universal laws without becoming unfree. If freedom is located in the individual and his selfish desires, then social life would appear possible only by setting up an external organisation to limit this freedom; government then appears as a necessary evil. But if men realise that their true freedom consists in the acceptance of principles, of laws which are their own, a synthesis of universal and particular interests becomes possible. It can be actualised, however, only in and through political institutions whereby the

[1] For the dialectical nature of this insight see S. Avineri, *The Social and Political Thought of Karl Marx*, Cambridge, 1968.

State proper is distinguished from civil society. Civil life then remains as an element of the State, but only as a subordinate moment of it. Political interests transcend but do not replace individual economic interests.

Marx's break with the Hegelian ideology of the State developed rapidly during 1843. Feuerbach's influence is very apparent in the manuscript Marx wrote on Hegel's Philosophy of the State in that year.[1]

In Feuerbach's *Preliminary Theses toward Reform of Philosophy* appears the idea that "we need only make the predicate into the subject and thus reverse speculative philosophy to arrive at the unconcealed pure truth". Marx took seriously this advice in his study of Hegel's *Philosophy of Right*, and this is no doubt the original source of Marx's notorious cryptic remark in the second edition of *Capital* about standing Hegel "on his head".

Similar points about the inversion of reality by German ideologists appear in Marx and Engels' *The German Ideology*. For example, the following jibe:

"First of all an abstraction is made from a fact; then it is declared that the fact is based on the abstraction. That is how to proceed if you want to appear German, profound and speculative.

For example: *Fact*: The cat eats the mouse.

Reflection: Cat = nature, mouse = nature, consumption of mouse by cat = consumption of nature by nature = self-consumption of nature.

Philosophic presentation of the fact: Devouring of the mouse by the cat is based upon the self-consumption of nature."[2]

A main theme of Marx's commentary on Hegel is that speculation reverses the roles of State and civil society. However, this is developed much more clearly in the two essays Marx published in the *Deutsch-Französische Jahrbücher* (1844), namely, *On the Jewish Question* and *Introduction to the Critique of Hegel's Philosophy of Right*, so we will move straight to an account of these.

---

[1] Parts of this appear in English translation in D. Easton and K. Guddat, eds., *Writings of the Young Marx on Philosophy and Society*, New York, 1967. See McLellan, *op. cit.*, for a detailed account of Feuerbach's influence.

[2] *The German Ideology*, London, 1965, p. 530.

Marx: On the Jewish Question

During the autumn of 1843 Marx composed *On the Jewish Question* which, in the form of a critique of Bruno Bauer, differentiates between "political emancipation" and "human emancipation", shows that civil society is the real basis of the State, and calls for the overcoming of the separation between them.[1]

In establishing these points Marx makes use of Feuerbach's term *species-being* as a key characterisation of man. For Feuerbach this refers primarily to man's consciousness of a "human essence" which is the same in himself and in other men, but Marx stresses more strongly than Feuerbach the social basis of this consciousness and the need to realise the potential of it in action by man as a *social* being.[2]

For Marx the free development of the potential inherent in mankind required the individual to think and act as a member of a universal community.

Now Marx followed Hegel in recognising that the life of "civil society", riven as it is by conflict (religious, economic, etc.), competition, egoism, in short a constellation of *private* interests, constitutes a kind of universality (in that individuals are brought into interconnection) but one which appears to the individual as an external *limit* to his freedom. The "others" appear to the individual of civil society as rivals, with conflicting interests, who circumscribe his freedom of action.

But, Marx argues further, contrary to Hegel, the modern State is unable to overcome the egoism of civil society and create a genuine community.

To understand this we must attend closely to what he says about *the nature of political emancipation*.

Political emancipation Marx characterises as the transformation of affairs of State from the *private* affairs of a ruler and his servants, separated from the people, into *public* affairs, matters of general concern to every citizen. However, this attempt to establish "fraternity" of citizens fails because of the *peculiar* nature of a merely *political* emancipation.

Marx argues that the modern State emancipates the Jews, not by freeing *them* from the domination of religion but by freeing *itself* from religion, by giving recognition to *no* religion and hence putting the Jews on an equal footing with everyone else. This is insufficient.

[1] For the influence of Moses Hess on Marx in this essay see McLellan *op. cit.*
[2] Cf. Thesis VI on Feuerbach.

"To be *politically* emancipated from religion is not to be finally and completely emancipated from religion, because political emancipation is not the final and absolute form of *human* emancipation."[1]

Marx goes on to generalise this conclusion for all bases of domination, conflict, and limitation.

". . . the state as a state abolishes *private property* (i.e. man decrees by *political* means the *abolition* of private property) when it abolishes the *property qualification* for voters and candidates, as has been done in many of the North American States. Hamilton interprets this phenomenon quite correctly from a political standpoint: *The masses have gained a victory over property owners and financial wealth.* Is not private property ideally abolished when the non-owner comes to legislate for the owner of property? The *property qualification* is the last *political* form in which private property is recognised. But the political suppression of private property not only does not abolish private property; it actually presupposes its existence. The state abolishes, after its fashion, the distinctions established by *birth, social rank, education, occupation,* when it decrees that birth, social rank, education, occupation are *non-political* distinctions; when it proclaims, without regard to these distinctions, that every member of society is an *equal* partner in popular sovereignty... Far from abolishing these *effective* differences, it only exists so far as they are presupposed. . . ."[2]

We see therefore that a partial, merely political, emancipation leaves intact the world of private interest, of domination and subordination, exploitation and competition, because the State establishes its universality, and the citizens their communality, only by abstracting away from the *real differences and interests* that separate the members of civil society and set them against one another. Hence Marx considers even the most perfect democratic state inadequate because it is based on this fundamental "contradiction between the political state and civil society".[3]

"[In] political democracy . . . man, not merely one man but every man, is there considered a sovereign being, a supreme being; but

---

[1] T. B. Bottomore, ed., *Karl Marx, Early Writings*, p. 10.
[2] *Early Writings*, pp. 11-12.
[3] *Ibid.,* p. 21 .

it is uneducated, un-social man, man just as he is in his fortuitous existence, man as he has been corrupted, lost to himself, alienated, subjected to the rule of inhuman conditions and elements, by the whole organisation of our society—in short man who is not yet a real species-being."[1]

Marx goes on to comment that political emancipation is the final form of human emancipation *within* the framework of the prevailing social order.

He develops further the theme of the opposition between the political state and civil society in a brilliant analysis of the meaning of the distinction between *political* rights, and the rights of man, so-called *natural* rights, as exemplified in the French and American Constitutions. He shows that the so-called natural and imprescriptible rights of liberty, of property, and of security, are not founded upon the relations between man and man, but rather on the separation of man from man. Liberty is defined in these constitutions simply as non-interference: "the limits within which each individual can act without harming others are determined by law, just as a boundary between two fields is marked by a stake".[2]

The right of property is, similarly, a right of self-interest. "It leads every man to see in other men, not the *realisation*, but rather the *limitation* of his own liberty."[3]

As for security: "security is the supreme social concept of civil society; the concept of the police. The whole society exists only in order to guarantee for each of its members the preservation of his person, his rights and his property".[4]

Marx concludes that, in these constitutions, "Species-life itself— society—appears as a system which is external to the individual and as a limitation of his original independence".[5] He finds it still more incomprehensible when it is declared that the political community is a mere *means* for preserving the so-called rights of man, thus making it appear "that it is man as a bourgeois and not man as a citizen who is considered the *true* and *authentic* man".[6]

That the private individual of civil society is considered by the existing constitutions as "true and authentic man" flows from the nature of the opposition between man as a citizen and as a member of civil society. The latter is man as he really is, with a certain occupation,

---

[1] *Early Writings*, p. 20.   [2] *Ibid.*, p. 24.   [3] *Ibid.*, p. 25.
[4] *Ibid.*, pp. 25–6.   [5] *Ibid.*, p. 26.   [6] *Ibid.*, p. 26.

amount of property, religious affiliation and so on, whereas "political man is only abstract, artificial man, man as an allegorical, moral person".[1]

Although Marx does not directly remark on it, we see here that the authors of bourgeois constitutions, however far they are below Hegel philosophically, are closer than he is to existing reality, for the latter's system establishes man as a universal being, a citizen, in the highest place.

Since Marx himself came from the Hegelian tradition, his inversion of the relation between the State and civil society as depicted by Hegel is of the highest importance, for it redirected his work from the critique of politics to a close study of civil society, of which he had done virtually no analysis up to then. This inversion was accomplished partly by a conceptual critique and partly simply by comparing Hegel's theory of the State with the facts of the existing State's behaviour.

The major point is that the peculiar way in which the modern state emancipates man by declaring that the real differences between men shall not affect their standing as citizens, and hence leaves these differences intact, not only leaves relations of domination and conflict in civil society untouched, but inevitably these real social relations infect the political sphere as well. The modern state, in contrast with feudalism, declares wealth, education, occupation, religion, race, in short all the real distinctions, *non-political* distinctions. Only in this way can it claim to stand for the *common* interests of the citizens. Yet how can wealth be unpolitical when it provides access to the means of political persuasion? Is the uneducated man in the same position as the educated one with respect to formulating meaningful policies? Are the political opportunities of the man of leisure the same as those of the harassed mother of six? Are race and religion unpolitical in a society full of prejudice and bigotry?

The unrepresentative character of so-called representative institutions —full of academics and businessmen—cannot be explained by the most minute examination of the constitutions, which unanimously declare every citizen of equal worth. It can only be explained by accepting that the State does not stand *above* society, but is *of* society; and this makes it necessary to analyse social life.

(We have only posed here some of the most obvious questions. One could go on to deal with the way social life conditions the ideological presuppositions of even well-meaning politicians.)

The fact that all the *real* attributes belong to the man of civil society, whereas the citizen, who is supposed to act in fraternity with his

[1] *Early Writings*, p. 30.

fellows, has been abstracted from all these real attributes, makes of the latter only a fiction of constitutions; hence civil life dominates political life. The solution, Marx concludes, will come when each man has recognised and organised his own powers as *social* powers so that he no longer separates the social power from himself as *political* power.

The solution must be seen not as a formal rejection of the State but as a dialectical solution to an immanent critique of the State taken at its face value.

For example—taking the question from the point of view of the State—it claims to represent the general interest. However, because of the way it has been set up it is powerless to enforce this if it wished. This is Marx's argument in an article a few months later than *On the Jewish Question*.

He points out that the State cannot transcend the contradiction between the aims and good intentions of the administration on the one hand and its means and resources on the other without transcending itself, for it is based on this contradiction. It must confine itself to a "formal and negative" activity because its power ceases where that of civil life begins. Consequently it is impotent to combat the unsocial consequences springing from the unsocial nature of civil society.[1]

Thus, if it is serious about enforcing the general interest, the State would have to absorb civil society and this, of course, would end its specific basis as an institution abstracted from civil life.

"At those times when the state is most aware of itself, political life seeks to stifle its own prerequisites—civil society and its elements —and to establish itself as the genuine and harmonious species-life of man. But it can only achieve this end by setting itself in *violent* contradiction with its own conditions of existence, by declaring a *permanent* revolution. Thus the political drama ends necessarily with the restoration of religion, of private property, of all the elements of civil society, just as war ends with the conclusion of peace."[2]

From the point of view of the citizen, also, a similar argument follows. If the modern state is to be truly representative of its citizens then the various disabilities of civil life which affect them politically must be removed, i.e. political emancipation must be backed up with

---

[1] *Critical Notes on "The King of Prussia and Social Reform"*. English Trans. D. Easton and K. Guddat; *Writings of the Young Marx on Philosophy and Society*, New York, 1967, pp. 348–9.

[2] *Early Writings*, p. 16.

social emancipation. But this in effect means a total "human emancipation" and destroys the basis of the political state established on a merely partial liberation.

It should not be thought that Marx was moved to reject the bourgeois ideology of the State by philosophical considerations only. From April 1842 until the censor closed the paper the following year, Marx, in articles in the *Rheinische Zeitung*, dealt with topical issues of the day. In these an increasing disillusionment with the behaviour of the government becomes evident. In one article in particular, on a wood-theft law depriving the peasants of their traditional right to collect kindling, he noted the State's harshness and injustice to the poor, in enforcing the interests of a particular class, the forest owners, rather than the interests of all.

The key advance made by Marx in 1843 was that, instead of trying to remedy such defects by reform of the State, he concluded that it was necessary to tackle the problem at its root by abolishing the presuppositions of the State. Having concluded that the real basis of the State was civil society the problem therefore boiled down to a transformation of the latter—to go beyond political emancipation to, what he called at this time, "human emancipation".

This critique of the State was concretised by Marx and Engels in *The German Ideology* and later writings. At this stage, in 1843, Marx had only got as far as "pointing the way" by shifting the focus of his critique from the State to civil society.

Introduction to the Critique of Hegel's Philosophy of Right

In the essay *On the Jewish Question* Marx does not even mention the proletariat. The call for "human emancipation" is not backed up by any analysis of what might be the historical agency of such an emancipation.

It is in the other essay that Marx published in the *Jahrbücher*, namely *Introduction to the Critique of Hegel's Philosophy of Right*, that he faces up to these questions and the proletariat takes its place for the first time at the heart of Marx's thinking—a position it never lost.

The main part of this essay is taken up with an acute analysis of the peculiar combination in Germany of theoretical advancement (in the shape of Hegelian and post-Hegelian philosophy) and political backwardness (as compared with modernising, revolutionary, nations like France). This posed an immediate problem for social critics like

Marx for "it is clear that the arm of criticism cannot replace the criticism of arms". He immediately hopefully qualifies this by stating that theory itself becomes a material force when it has seized the masses. Nevertheless the problem remains that revolutions need "a *passive* element, a *material* basis. Theory is only realised in a people so far as it fulfils the needs of the people. . . . Will theoretical needs be directly practical needs? It is not enough that thought should seek to realise itself; reality must strive towards thought".[1]

The search for a real force in social life to realise the demands posed by his theoretical critique becomes connected, for Marx, with the distinction between "universal emancipation" and a "partial, merely political, revolution".

He sees the basis of partial revolution in that a particular class frees itself, and hence society in general, from the limitations imposed by certain privileges held by another class. But in so far as the class carrying through the emancipation has class interests based on its *own* particular place in civil society, e.g. that it possesses or can easily acquire, money or culture, it will cease its radical efforts at the point at which the field is free for the people sharing this *particular situation* to advance themselves.

Marx argues that no class in Germany has the courage to carry through such a partial emancipation. It follows therefore that emancipation can only be achieved by a class *forced* to it by its immediate situation, by material necessity. Emancipation will thus be total and not partial in Germany, because it will be made by a class with no *particular* claims, but one acting from the desperation of total deprivation. In short, a *universal class*.

"A class must be formed which has *radical chains*, a class in civil society which is not a class of civil society, a class which is the dissolution of all classes, a sphere of society which has a universal character because its sufferings are universal . . ., which is, in short, a *total loss* of humanity and which can only redeem itself by a *total redemption of humanity*. This dissolution of society, as a particular class, is the *proletariat*.[2]

That is, because the situation of the proletariat is so desperate that it has nothing to lose by revolution, it has no special interests in the existing order to protect. Therefore it can only free itself by establishing *universal* freedom, by overthrowing *all* existing bases of oppression.

[1] *Early Writings*, pp. 52–4.   [2] *Early Writings*, p. 58.

This is the class which is capable of being as radical in practice as the development of post-Hegelian criticism of society has become in theory.

Marx sums up by proclaiming: "philosophy can only be realised by the abolition of the proletariat, and the proletariat can only be abolished by the realisation of philosophy."[2]

Here, then, Marx's philosophical development makes its historic rendezvous with the proletariat.

At this point Marx's development is in a transitional stage between idealism and materialism. He is handling "the realisation of philosophy" and the "material basis", i.e. the proletariat, as separate—though requiring each other to complete their development. He has not yet achieved a coherent account of the interdependence of theory and practice in a dialectically conceived totality—such as he sketches in the *Theses On Feuerbach* (1845).

His next step is clear—an analysis of "civil society" and the condition of the proletariat. That Marx undertook this in the shape of a study of *political economy* is in no small measure due to Engels.

Outlines of a Critique of Political Economy

Although Engels was indisputably the lesser talent of the partnership, as he himself modestly acknowledged, there is sometimes evidenced a tendency to reduce his role to nil, which is not only unfair to him but does a disservice to Marx. Marx was never one to judge lightly the intellectual deficiencies of others, yet of all his contemporaries it was with Engels he chose to form a close intellectual partnership in 1844-45. Apart from their general agreement on the inadequacies of German idealism, the prime cause of Marx's high opinion of Engels was the material the latter published in the *Deutsch-Französische Jahrbücher* of 1844 (in which the two essays by Marx analysed above also appeared).

As late as the famous *Preface* to *A Contribution to the Critique of Political Economy*, 1859, Marx still refers very favourably to the essay by Engels, *Outlines of a Critique of Political Economy*, which sparked off their correspondence and collaboration.

In this essay Engels refutes Malthus, pointing out, amongst other things, the possibility through science of revolutionising the productivity of the soil. But perhaps the most significant point from the point of view of the future development of Marxism was his interest in the trade cycle.

[2] *Early Writings*, p. 59.

"What are we to think of a law which can only assert itself through periodic crises? It is just a natural law based on the unconsciousness of the participants. . . . Produce with consciousness as human beings—not as dispersed atoms without consciousness of your species—and you are beyond all these artificial and untenable antitheses. But as long as you continue to produce in the present unconscious thoughtless manner, at the mercy of chance—for just so long trade crises will remain; and each successive crisis is bound to become more universal . . . finally causing a social revolution such as has never been dreamt of by the school wisdom of the economists."[1]

While Engels went on to produce his book *Conditions of the Working Class in England in 1844*, Marx, too, threw himself into the study of political economy, bringing to it the conceptual framework he had developed out of German philosophy.

Economic and Philosophic Manuscripts of 1844

In the last decade these early writings by Marx have become justly famous for their employment of the category of *Alienation*. This term has been taken up by so many writers, in so many contexts, it no longer has a stable meaning. However, if one was to attempt a rough definition useful from the point of view of Marxian studies, one could say that alienation was a process whereby a subject suffers from dependence upon an apparently external agency that was originally his own product.

The Young Hegelians took over the term from Hegel's metaphysics and gave it a more concrete employment, particularly in the critique of religion and theology. In Feuerbach, for example, one might say that the message is: "Man created God in his own image and then treated himself as dependent on his own creation."

Marx starts by treating the State as another such form of alienation of man from his "species", but in 1844 roots the whole concept in the labour process. In his 1844 critique of political economy "alienated labour" is the key organising concept.

Since mountains of literature have been produced on the subject I shall try to be brief here. According to Marx, labour's product "confronts it as *something alien*, as a *power independent* of the producers". Because the product is only "congealed" labour this therefore means

---

[1] *Outlines of a Critique of Political Economy;* appended to K. Marx, *Economic and Philosophical Manuscripts of 1844,* Lawrence and Wishart, London, 1959, p. 196.

that "in the conditions dealt with by political economy" labour can only appear as "estrangement, as alienation".

What Marx seems to have in mind in the *Manuscripts* is, chiefly, the relation of labour to capital, judging from such passages as the following:

> "All these consequences are contained in the definition that the worker is related to the *product of his labour* as to an *alien* object. For on this premise it is clear that the more the worker spends himself, the more powerful the alien objective world becomes which he creates over against himself, the poorer he himself—his inner world—becomes, the less belongs to him as his own."[1]

To understand this, let us ask ourselves why the worker is in his miserable condition, forced to obey the boss? The answer seems to be—because he has nothing to sell but his labour power, while the boss is the owner of capital. But how does the capitalist maintain, and even increase, his store of capital? The answer can only be— through the labour of the workers. That is, the more the worker produces, the more surplus-value is realised by the capitalist when he sells the products, and hence the greater his store of capital and domination over the worker. Capital itself is only 'objectified' labour. Thus we see that the workers, in effect, continually *reproduce the conditions of their subservience*. This is what makes their situation an alienated and alienating one—whereas simple robbery, based on brute force, would not be.

Here the product reappears as capital, but in *The German Ideology* Marx and Engels seem to employ alienation, or estrangement, most often in connection with the product as it appears on the commodity market (see pp. 53-56).

Both themes reappear in *Capital*, though with a greater precision of concepts and quantitative treatment; the former in the analysis of the secret of capitalist profit, and the latter in such passages as Chapter One, section 4, *Commodity Fetishism*, in which the subservience of the producers to the laws of the commodity market is compared to the superstition of a savage who fashions a fetish with his own hand and then falls down and worships it.

Following the treatment of the "alienation of the worker in his product" Marx, in the *1844 Manuscripts*, develops the theme of the alienation of labour itself.

---

[1] *Economic and Philosophic Manuscripts of 1844*, p. 70.

"If then the product of labour is alienation, production itself must be active alienation, the alienation of activity, the activity of alienation. . . . Labour is *external* to the worker, i.e. it does not belong to his essential being; . . . in his work therefore, he does not affirm himself but denies himself, does not feel content but unhappy, does not develop freely his mental and physical energy but mortifies his body and ruins his mind."[1]

Without developing the further ramifications of this idea I want to move straight on to consideration of a problem with important implications—what is the relationship between alienated labour and private property?

If one asks for the *reason* why the worker is in such a miserable situation, in which his product, and even his very activity, belong to someone else, in which he cannot find satisfaction in his work and his product, but on the contrary experiences these as alien, as hostile; it might seem that it is the rule of private property or more specifically Capital, that is to blame.

However, there is one snag in defining the relation in terms of private property as cause and alienated labour as effect—Marx said exactly the opposite. It is worth quoting the whole passage:

"The relationship of the worker to labour engenders the relationship to it of the capitalist. . . . Private property is thus the product, the result, the necessary consequence, of alienated labour, of the external relation of the worker to nature and to himself.

Private property thus results by analysis from the concept of alienated labour, i.e. of alienated man. . . .

True it is as a result of the movement of private property that we have obtained the concept of alienated labour from political economy. But on analysis of this concept it becomes clear that though private property appears to be the source, the cause of alienated labour, it is really its consequence, just as the gods *in the beginning* are not the cause but the effect of man's intellectual confusion. Later this relationship becomes reciprocal."[2]

Why does Marx want to make private property the product of alienated labour? Why not, for example, taking up the point about reciprocity, treat it as a chicken and egg question, say that private property and alienated labour are mutually necessary conditions?

[1] *Economic and Philosophic Manuscripts of 1844*, p. 72.   [2] *Ibid.*, p. 80.

That is, say that lack of private property forces workers to alienate their labour, but that private property in its turn, grows on the tribute it exacts from wage labour.

Certainly the difficulty of imagining alienated labour *in isolation* from private property makes it impossible that Marx could mean that the former was historically prior to the latter. Indeed in his analysis of the origins of capitalism he stresses the *two* necessary conditions—a mass of wealth accumulated and a mass of landless vagabonds with nothing to sell but their labour power.

No, as in the first few chapters of *Capital*, it is clear that Marx is giving a structural analysis of a given whole here, rather than considering the origins of the system. In this given whole Marx discerns two aspects, private property and alienated labour, but the secret of why he intends to make the latter fundamental and the former a function of it, can be found a page or two later when he remarks:

"When one speaks of private property, one thinks of being concerned with something external to man. When one speaks of labour, one is directly concerned with man himself."[1]

That is to say, the question with Marx in all his work is how to penetrate beneath the abstract categories of political economy and social life generally, to the human reality underlying them; and then in turn to exhibit the meaning of these apparently self-subsistent spheres and categories in terms of human activity.

To invert this relationship and derive forms of human activity from categories external to it, whether from God in religion, or from the Absolute Idea in Hegel, or from private property as in so many political economists, is a procedure which itself is typical of an estranged form of consciousness. To attribute powers to private property, to make it the subject which originates activity and to make man himself merely its object, is pure superstition. It is to reify an abstract category, that is to say, treat it as a thing in itself and attribute powers to it that properly belong to human beings.

In the original passage quoted above it is noteworthy that Marx illuminates this way of thinking by comparing it with religion—"The gods in the beginning are not the cause but the effect of man's intellectual confusion."

This recalls Feuerbach's materialist critique of religion where he argues that men have created God in their own idealised image and

[1] *Economic and Philosophic Manuscripts of 1844*, p. 82.

then treated their own creation as their lord and master and fallen down before it.

In the same way, Marx argues, private property must be understood as a creation of human activity, a form of social life, not as an eternal self-subsistent entity. If it appears—and not just in theoretical speculation, but also in the experience of millions—as dominating man himself, then it must be due to a very peculiar *alienating* activity which results in the *products* of human activity appearing as alien hostile beings. Marx generalises this conclusion as follows:

"Just as we have found the concept of private property from the concept of estranged labour by analysis, in the same way every category of political economy can be evolved with the help of these two factors; and we shall find again in each category, e.g. trade, competition, capital, money, only a definite and developed expression of the first foundation."[1]

Of course, as Marx allows, this kind of analysis still leaves over the problem of the roots of this estrangement in the process of human development; but unfortunately the manuscript breaks off unfinished before he begins to answer this question.

It is in *The German Ideology* that Marx and Engels provide an *historical* account of labour and property. Once again the legal category, property, is taken by them as less fundamental than labour. They argue that the different forms of ownership are determined by the development in the *division of labour*.[2] The historical place of alienation is also located in this development.[3]

The Holy Family

In July 1844 Engels visited Marx in Paris and they agreed to collaborate on a critique of the Young Hegelians—which appeared as *The Holy Family* in 1845. In truth most of it was written by Marx and while much of the detailed analysis of Bauer and Co. is of little interest today we do find hints of themes which retain a permanent place in their later work. For example, the following passage is a splendid example of the fruitful use of the dialectical approach.

"Proletariat and wealth are antitheses. As such they form a whole. They are both formations of the world of private property. What concerns us here is to define the particular position they take

[1] *Economic and Philosophic Manuscripts of 1844*, p. 82.
[2] See, e.g., p. 43.　　　[3] See pp. 53-56.

within the opposition. It is not enough to say that they are two sides of a whole. Private property, as private property, as wealth, is forced to maintain its own existence and thereby the existence of its opposite, the proletariat. It is the positive side of the opposition, private property satisfied in itself.

The proletariat, on the other hand, is forced, as proletariat, to abolish itself, and with this, its antithesis, the condition which makes it a proletariat—private property. It is the negative side of the contradiction, its principle of unrest, private property dissolved and in process of dissolution.

The propertied class and the proletarian class express the same human alienation. But the former feels comfortable and confirmed in it, recognises this self-alienation as *its own power* and thus has the *semblance* of a human existence. The latter feels itself crushed by this alienation, sees in it its own impotence and the reality of an inhuman existence. It is, to use an expression of Hegel's, 'in the midst of degradation the *revolt* against degradation', a revolt to which it is forced by the contradiction between its *humanity* and its situation, which is an open, clear, and absolute negation of its humanity.

Within this antithesis, therefore, the property owner is the *conservative* and the proletarian the *destructive* party.

In its economic movement private property drives on to its own dissolution, but only through a development which is independent of it, unconscious, achieved against its will, and brought about by the very nature of things—that is by producing the proletariat *as* proletariat, poverty conscious of its spiritual and physical poverty, dehumanisation conscious of its dehumanisation and thus transcending itself. The proletariat carries out the sentence which private property, by creating the proletariat, passes upon itself just as it carries out the sentence which wage-labour passes upon itself by creating wealth for others and poverty for itself. If the proletariat triumphs, this does not mean that it becomes the absolute side of society, for it is victorious only by abolishing itself and its opposite. Then both the proletariat and the opposite which conditions it, private property, disappear." (Chap. 4.)

The German Ideology

All of this early work, the turn towards materialism, the critique of the State, the realisation of the importance of civil society and hence of political economy, bore splendid fruit when in 1845-46 Marx and Engels achieved a synthetic world outlook, later called historical materialism, set out in Part One of *The German Ideology* and the *Theses on Feuerbach* from the same period. Up to this time Marx and Engels would not have been considered by their contemporaries as especially different from Feuerbach or Hess—but the breakthrough represented by *The German Ideology* marks them off finally from their German philosophical past and also from all varieties of socialism and communism current at the time. It goes without saying that even after 1846 almost everything remained still to be done—the important thing is that the groundwork for a conceptual framework mapping out a whole line of march, with almost endless possibilities, is here indicated.

If one was to single out the most fundamental idea in *The German Ideology*, which is discovered in the *1844 Manuscripts* and is assumed by *Capital*, it would be that *man produces himself through labour.* He has neither a fixed unchanging nature, purely biologically determined (as a present-day trend of obviously conservative implications would have it); but neither does he develop himself in accordance with some spiritual essence, as so many idealists have pretended. There is rather a dialectically conceived relation between his nature as determined by the conditions of his life, and the practical transformation of those conditions. The link between the two is labour—in its broadest sense.

It follows that one cannot speak of "Man" as such, except at a highly abstract level. History is made by particular kinds of men, with specific needs and problems, and specific conditions of life determining the possibility of a solution to those problems.

Some of the implications of these fundamental principles are sketched by Marx and Engels in the first part of *The German Ideology*. The account above of the intellectual evolution of the authors should enable the reader to follow the work without further comment on it here. However, it might be as well to warn against one common misinterpretation. It is possible to select certain one-sided formulations, which the authors no doubt resorted to for the purpose of contrasting forcibly their positions from those of the dominant idealist trends, and make these the basis of a fatalistic view which negates human purposefulness and activity. This kind of view is sometimes referred to as "mechanistic materialism", since its categories are homologous with those with which natural science treats its objects.

A careful reading of Marx's work soon shows that this interpretation is not adequate; because the circumstances which are held to shape and form consciousness are not independent of human activity. They are precisely the *social* relations which have been *historically* created by human action. Hence the importance of "practice" in Marx's work.

On the occasions when he had to deal with other materialists Marx was always careful to mark himself off from them, as we see in the *Theses on Feuerbach* in this volume. In Thesis One he is even prepared to give some credit to idealism as against the aforementioned mechanistic materialism. A close analysis of the third thesis, however, will bring out my point best. This reads:

"The materialist doctrine concerning the changing of circumstances and upbringing forgets that circumstances are changed by men and that it is essential to educate the educator himself. This doctrine must, therefore, divide society into two parts, one of which is superior to society.

The coincidence of the changing of circumstances and of human activity or self-changing can be conceived and rationally understood only as *revolutionary practice*."

Now the view that Marx is criticising here is clearly that which sees in social life nothing but the production of people by their circumstances. These tendencies were materialist enough to see that it was ridiculous to blame people for being as they were when their circumstances and education had conditioned this. The solution, clearly enough, was to provide better circumstances and a decent upbringing and hence produce better people. Marx's complaint is that this leaves unexplained the transition from the first situation to the second. These tendencies (Engels cites Owen as an example in his edition of the *Theses*) are inconsistent in that they do not critically examine the basis of *their own* activity. Inconsistently, they say that people are nothing but passive products of circumstances, while their own activity is implicitly based upon a rational insight into the nature of the ideal society and purposive action of some kind to bring about change. They do not notice that their proposition about circumstances producing men has only half the truth, and conversely they do not see that the educators, who are to be called in to mould the new men, must themselves have been produced by given circumstances and education.

Marx wants to say that *all* men are both products of circumstances and potential changers of circumstances. Instead of trying to comprehend how this might be, the tendency he is criticising splits the process of change into two. First someone "superior to society" sets up certain circumstances and education, and then the mass of the people are produced as new men by those circumstances. Marx, however, insisted on a more dialectical relation between circumstances and activity which must be grasped as "revolutionary practice".

One might ask why, if Marx does justice to both sides, he calls himself a materialist instead of something more neutral? The answer can only be that any Marxian attempt to resolve the apparent antithesis between mechanical determination and self-conscious activity must include the point that *in the first instance* material circumstances condition us, however much we revolutionise those conditions later. We cannot create our being by some undetermined pure act. We have to be *produced* as living substantial beings before we can begin to act. This is true both of the individual and the species. The individual cannot determine the historical period or the class he is born into—which fundamentally limits his possibilities. The species itself at the dawn of history already had a certain mode of life before it could begin to recreate itself through solving the problems which faced it with solutions also conditioned by the given circumstances.

Nevertheless one can see clearly both in the *Theses* and *The German Ideology* that Marx's materialism does comprehend "revolutionary practice"—and this gives it a dynamic edge, lacking in the models which one-sidedly abstract from history the aspect of passive determination.

The German Ideology and Stirner

Part II of *The German Ideology*, following a short excursion against Bauer, is entirely devoted to an attack on Max Stirner. The last part is an attack on "True" socialism.

No less than two-thirds of the whole book is taken up by the detailed line by line critique of Stirner's book *The Ego and Its Own*. The weight given to his views, of little interest now except as foreshadowing anarchism, reflects the importance they had at the time. Stirner prided himself on being the most extreme of the Young Hegelians. Everyone else, Bauer, Feuerbach, Marx, etc., he believed to have escaped one superstition only to fall under the spell of another.

All the tendencies attacked by Stirner felt constrained to reply, while the space Marx and Engels devote to him seems to show that they considered him the most dangerous enemy of socialist thought at the time.

David McLellan in his excellent work *The Young Hegelians and Karl Marx* has argued persuasively that Stirner's impact on Marx has been underestimated. Usually Feuerbach is given as the last influence on Marx and Engels before they struck out on their own. However, this is chronologically incorrect because Stirner's work appeared *after* Feuerbach's influential works. Furthermore, McLellan argues that the impact of Stirner's scorching attack on Feuerbach's humanism speeded Marx and Engels' own divergence from the latter—as well as from the types of ethical socialism ridiculed by Stirner.

Marx and Engels are rather unfair to Stirner in that they sometimes criticise him along the lines—"Stirner says communists believe X whereas they really believe Y". In truth at the time Stirner wrote it could be shown that socialists—for example the "true" socialists— *did* believe X, whereas Y is often something Marx and Engels had only just developed (perhaps in *response* to Stirner's criticism) and of which Stirner could not therefore have been expected to take cognizance.

There is little that Marx took directly from Stirner—except possibly his iconoclasm in respect of ethical invocations—but the polemic with him doubtless helped to clarify his mind on many questions.

In order to give readers an idea of the main themes of the parts of *The German Ideology* left out in this edition we will now rehearse them.

The Critique of Stirner

Stirner (the pseudonym of Kaspar Schmidt) prided himself on being the boldest of all the Young Hegelians. His book *Der Einzige und sein Eigentum* appeared in 1844 and carried to an extreme their rejection of anything religious. To Stirner all "causes" were only different manifestations of "the Holy" except "his own cause". He declared that he refused to enrol himself in the service of God, the State, the nation, humanity, truth, love or justice. He would consider only his own Ego—all the other values were only abstractions—fetishes no more worthy of respect than the objects of religious superstition. "Only I am not an abstraction."

Because Stirner saw "the Holy" everywhere he looked, Marx and Engels lampoon him as a "Saint" and erect an elaborate structure based on this idea within which their critique is expressed.

Before looking at this critique of Stirner it is worth saying a word about the latter's attack on Feuerbach, which was the most influential part of his book.

In *Das Wesen des Christentums* Feuerbach presented an anthropo-morphic critique of religion. In religion man saw his alienated essence in a metaphysical disguise. It was only necessary to understand that behind this disguise stood man himself in order to grasp the real meaning of religion.

In this Feuerbach uses his transformational method of reversing subject and predicate. Thus Love is not holy because it is a predicate of God, but people attribute it to God because it is divine by itself. But Love is a *human* quality: Feuerbach therefore suggested that the theological entity should be thrown out and a new humanist religion based on Love established.

For Stirner, however, "humanity" was just as much an abstraction as "God". To change religious commands into moral ones still leaves us enslaved to ideals that stand above and apart from the Ego—which finds all general principles alien since each and every Ego is "unique". Stirner comments that it was not much use Feuerbach transposing subject and predicates if he is going to worship the predicates. Stirner's neurotic iconoclasm is noted by Marx and Engels in the following passage.

"Incidentally, as regards the source of Saint Max's hatred of 'predicates', he himself gives an extremely naïve disclosure in the 'Apologetic Commentary'. He quotes the following passage from *Das Wesen des Christentums* (p. 31): 'A true atheist is only one for whom the *predicates* of divine essence, e.g. love, wisdom, justice, are nothing, but not one for whom only the *subject* of these predi-cates is nothing'—and then he exclaims triumphantly: '*Does this not hold good for Stirner?*'—'Here is wisdom'. In the above passage Saint Max found a hint as to how one should start in order to go '*farthest of all*'. He believes Feuerbach that the above passage reveals the 'essence' of the '*true atheist*', and lets Feuerbach set him the 'task' of becoming a 'true atheist'. The 'Unique' is the '*true atheist*'."[1]

Half of Stirner's work is taken up with a pseudo-historical "develop-ment" in the Hegelian manner, complete with triads, designed to present his "unique" egoism as the culmination of world history. In fact Stirner was weak on history and Marx and Engels spend a lot of time sneering at his mistakes. They have no difficulty in showing that Stirner operates with only two basic categories, "spirit" and "corpo-reality" which are simply dressed up in various disguises throughout

[1] Marx and Engels, *The German Ideology*, London, 1965, p. 256.

his schemas. Stirner's egoism is supposed to be their "negative unity", in which he is enslaved neither by things nor thoughts but incorporates both in himself. The bad logic and etymological tricks that he resorts to in achieving this result are laboriously investigated by the authors.

As far as the modern age is concerned this is dominated by "spirit", thinks Stirner, according to the following summary by Marx and Engels:

> "The consistent conclusion—which has already appeared again and again—of Stirner's view of history is as follows: 'Concepts should regulate life, concepts should rule. That is the religious world to which Hegel gave systematic expression' (p. 126), and which our good-natured philistine so much mistakes for the real world that on the following page 127 he can say: 'Now nothing but spirit rules in the world.' "[1]

Thus Stirner analyses the modern world in terms of a demonology of the spirits to which we are enslaved. The authors argue that this is a gross misunderstanding, e.g. where Stirner sees nothing but the domination of "the Holy" in the family, they point out the entirely material basis of the family.[2]

Generally speaking, the authors argue, Stirner's "history" says nothing about real life but presents the whole development in terms of variations in consciousness, and mainly the consciousness of the philosophers at that. Stirner does not concern himself with the physical and social changes taking place which produce an altered consciousness in the individual. For him people always find the world ready-made: "absolutely nothing is done to ensure that anything at all could be found".[3]

Instead of treating of real relations Stirner takes the distorted expression of these in ideology to be the real substance of history, and thus produces only "phrases about phrases". This idealist approach dictates the nature of Stirner's "struggles". In spite of their earth-shaking language his prescriptions turn out on examination simply to involve a change in the *attitude* of the Ego to these "ruling concepts", leaving everything as it is, "changing only his conception, and that not even of things, but of philosophical phrases about things".[4]

Marx and Engels show the ludicrousness of this approach in discussing Stirner's advice to the proletariat. He finds the secret of economics in

---

[1] Marx and Engels, *The German Ideology*, London, 1965, p. 203.
[2] *Ibid.*, p. 191–3.   [3] *Ibid.*, p. 132.   [4] *Ibid.*, p. 205.

the fact that "burghers and workers believe in the 'truth' of money". The authors charge that he thereby seems to think that he can abolish the "truth of money" in the same way as he abolishes in his mind the "truth" of God or of Hegelian philosophy. They argue that Stirner does not realise that money is a necessary product of definite relations of production and intercourse and remains a "truth" as long as these relations exist.[1]

Stirner's second discovery is that the workers "have only to cease work and to regard what they have produced by their labour as their property and to enjoy it". Marx and Engels comment trenchantly:

"As he did above in the case of money, here again our good burgher transforms the workers, who are scattered throughout the civilised world into a closed society which has only to adopt a decision in order to get rid of all difficulties. Saint Max does not know, of course, that merely since 1830 in England at least fifty attempts have been made, and at the present moment yet another is being made, to gather all the workers, of England alone, into a single association and that highly empirical causes have frustrated the success of all these projects. He does not know that even a minority of these workers, if they united to cease work, would very soon find themselves compelled to act in a revolutionary way. . . ."[2]

In sum, Stirner, in spite of his criticism of Feuerbach's retention of the religious attitude, is even more credulous than the latter. He faithfully accepts the Feuerbachian predicates (mentioned above) as real personalities ruling the world. He attaches the predicate "holy" to them,

"*transforming this predicate into a subject*, the 'Holy', i.e. doing exactly the same as that for which he reproaches Feuerbach. And so, after he has thus completely got rid of the definite content that was the matter at issue, he begins his struggle, i.e. he discloses his 'ill will' against this 'Holy' which, of course, always remains the same. Feuerbach has still—for which Saint Max reproaches him—the consciousness 'that for him it is "only a matter of destroying an illusion"' (p. 77 of the 'Book'), although Feuerbach still attaches much too great importance to the struggle against this illusion. In 'Stirner' even this consciousness has 'all gone', he actually believes

---

[1] Marx and Engels, *The German Ideology*, London, 1965, p. 218.
[2] *Ibid.*, p. 219.

in the domination of the abstract ideas of ideology in the modern world; he believes that in his struggle against 'predicates', against conceptions, he is no longer attacking an illusion, but the real forces that rule the world."[1]

Stirner appears as an iconoclastic realist because he denies abstractions their "truth", but he still believes that up until now these abstractions have *ruled*. He fails to comprehend the reality behind the illusions, so ends by taking these illusions at close to their face value. Therefore he thinks it sufficient to reject these ideas without realising this does not touch the real powers behind them, i.e. the *actual* State, Prince, etc.

Stirner sees the State as one of his worst enemies, for it opposes his will with an alien one. He even decides that all property is "State property" which the State only transfers to the capitalists "in feudal possession". Marx and Engels, of course, reverse this relationship of dependence between property and the State.

At the same time as he overestimates the power of the State he underestimates it when it comes to getting rid of it. "The State owes its existence only to the contempt which I have for myself", and "with the disappearance of this disdain it will totally die out."[2]

It could hardly be clearer how idealist Stirner's conception is—that simply changing one's *ideas* about one's relation to the State would be sufficient to dispose of its real power.

In the same way Stirner attacks "holy property" and points out that people should have "borne in mind that large property also belongs to them", then "they would not have respectfully excluded themselves from it and would not have been excluded".

Marx and Engels counter this by stressing that private property is "a form of intercourse necessary for certain stages of development of the productive forces" and has nothing to do with "respect" or "disrespect".[3]

Stirner criticises Communism for wanting to sacrifice the "Ego" to a "holy society". The general line of Marx and Engels' counter-critique is that Stirner's description of communism is not real communism but only the bourgeois caricature of communism, including notions such as "duty", "equal rights", "equal wages", etc., which are only modulations of the categories appertaining to bourgeois society.

[1] Marx and Engels, *The German Ideology*, London, 1965, p. 255–6.
[2] Stirner: quoted *The German Ideology*, p. 378.
[3] *The German Ideology*, p. 386.

Stirner also argues that "a society cannot be made new so long as those of whom it consists and who constitute it, remain as old". The authors reply to this:

"Stirner believes that the communist proletarians who revolutionise society and put the relations of production and the form of intercourse on a new basis—i.e. on themselves as new people, on their new mode of life—that these proletarians remain 'as of old'. The tireless propaganda carried out by these proletarians, their daily discussions among themselves, sufficiently prove how little they want people to remain 'as of old'. They would only remain 'as of old' if, with Sancho, they 'sought the blame in themselves'; but they know too well that only under changed circumstances will they cease to be 'as of old', and therefore they are determined to change these circumstances at the first opportunity. In revolutionary activity the changing of oneself coincides with the changing of circumstances."[1]

On the question of equal rights Stirner bases himself on the assertion that rights without the power to enforce them are empty so the only thing of importance is how much power one has. He therefore denies that equal work gives the right to equal enjoyment: only by "seizing" enjoyment will you actually get it. On this Marx and Engels comment:

"Saint Sancho again presents the proletarians here as a 'closed society', which has only to take the decision of 'seizing' in order the next day to put a summary end to the existing world order. But in reality the proletarians arrive at this unity only through a long process of development in which the appeal to this right also plays a part. Incidentally, this appeal to their right is only a means of making them take shape as 'they', as a revolutionary, united, mass."[2]

This remark is rather interesting because it might be held that in some later writings Marx underestimates the role played by the "appeal to right" in his anxiety to combat non-materialist, ethically based socialist theories.

In spite of Stirner's "egoism" he too is forced by the facts to admit that he has to relate to other people, and he describes such a set-up as

[1] *The German Ideology*, p. 229-30.   [2] *Ibid.*, p. 350-1.

an "Association of Egoists". However, Marx and Engels argue that because he has not, in his critique of existing society, gone beyond ideas to real relations he necessarily reproduces in the "Association" all these relations—the only thing that is changed is the "point of view" from which they are "regarded". Everything that was previously represented as an imposition of the "Holy" is now presented as due to "agreement". He accordingly presents a judicial fiction whereby his exclusion from the property of others is regarded as being the result of his coming to an agreement with these others, and reaches the astounding position that "I *see* nothing alien in the wealth belonging to the banker".[1]

Stirner is very anxious to establish his "uniqueness" by claiming that he by no means provides a philosophical apologia for "ordinary egoism". His egoism is "extraordinary" and is in fact the "negative unity" of the dialectical contradiction between the ordinary egoists and the "self-sacrificers". In order to establish this he has to prove to the latter that they are really egoists and to the ordinary egoists that they are really self-sacrificers.

Marx and Engels point out that the trick of proving to the altruists that they are really egoists, doing as they do for their own pleasure, is an old dodge already exploited by Bentham and others. Stirner's "unique" contribution is to prove to the egoists that they really sacrifice themselves. He does this mainly by trying to prove to them that they are in the service of various "fixed ideas", on the analogy of the miser, and pointing out that in history "private interests" have always been subordinated to "general or ideal interests".

Stirner's "egoist in the extraordinary sense" has to carry on a terrible struggle in order to avoid being "owned" by his passions, interests, tasks, ideas, vocation, etc. etc. He dare not entertain any purpose or desire for fear of being struck down by an alien determination. Marx and Engels laboriously follow him through all these bogs and thickets with the tenacity of bull-terriers and show the infinite regress involved in such a metaphysical psychology. It is perhaps worth quoting *in extenso* a passage where they analyse the nature of the tasks set for people, according to Stirner by "the Holy", and for Marx and Engels by their needs and conditions:

". . . our saint's favourite manoeuvre is the exploitation of the words destiny, vocation, task, etc., by which means it becomes

[1] Quoted *The German Ideology*, p. 444.

infinitely easy for him to transform whatever he likes into the Holy. For in vocation, destiny, task, etc., the individual appears in his own imagination as something different from what he actually is, as the Alien, hence as the Holy, and he advances his idea of what he ought to be as the Rightful, the Ideal, the Holy, in opposition to his real being. . . .

And now, of course, it only remains for him [Stirner] zealously to admonish people to select for themselves the destiny of absence of any destiny, the vocation of absence of any vocation, the task of absence of any task. . . .

The proletarian, for example, who like every other person is called upon to satisfy his needs and who is not in a position to satisfy even the needs that he has in common with other people . . . this proletarian if only for these reasons is confronted with the real task of revolutionising his conditions. He can, of course, imagine this to be his 'vocation', he can also, if he likes to engage in propaganda, express his 'vocation' by saying that to do this or that is the human vocation of the proletarian, the more so since his position does not even allow him to satisfy the needs arising directly from his human nature. Saint Sancho does not concern himself with the reality underlying this idea, with the practical aim of the proletarian —he clings fast to the work 'vocation' and declares it to be the Holy, and the proletarian to be the servant of the Holy—the easiest way of considering himself superior and 'proceeding further'.

Particularly in the conditions that have existed hitherto, when one class always ruled, when the conditions of life of an individual always coincided with the conditions of life of a class, when, therefore, the practical task of each newly rising class was bound to appear to each of its members a *universal* task, and when each class could overthrow its predecessor only by liberating the individuals of *all* classes from particular chains which had hitherto fettered them—under these circumstances it was essential that the task of the individual members of a class striving for domination should be depicted as a universal human task.

Incidentally, if for example the bourgeois tells the proletarian that his, the proletarian's, human task is to work fourteen hours a day, then the proletarian is quite justified in replying in the same language that on the contrary his task is to overthrow the entire bourgeois system. . . .

The all-round development of the individual will only cease to be conceived as ideal, as vocation, etc. when the impact of the world which stimulates the real development of the abilities of the individual comes under the control of the individuals themselves, as the communists desire."[1]

Even more interesting and important is the alternative solution Marx and Engels give for moral problems such as Stirner's conflict between egoism and self-sacrifice. In the brief critique of Bauer at the beginning of this part of *The German Ideology* they had noted that Bauer gets into trouble because "he does not forsake the speculative basis in order to solve the contradictions of speculation". In a similar way, in the example under discussion the authors argue that if we can understand the material basis of such moral conflicts then we can grasp the conditions under which a solution could be accomplished. Stirner, of course, claims that communists belong to the camp of the "self-sacrificers". Marx and Engels argue that communism does not preach such a morality; neither does it try to construct in abstraction a fictitious synthesis as Stirner does; rather communism changes the basis of the problem and provides, not another moral "ought" to counterpose to these others, but a demonstration that with the materially determined transformation of the present conditions of life, the expression of these conditions in ideological contradictions "disappears of itself".

Finally, in spite of Stirner's abjuring of "abstractions" it is perfectly clear that his "Ego" is itself an abstraction from the complex unity of social life.

As well as demonstrating the theoretical confusions of Stirner's thought Marx and Engels also provide a sketch of its roots in petit-bourgeois illusions very prevalent in a Germany relatively backward in its economic development.

True Socialism

The last section of *The German Ideology* concerns the "true" socialists. Marx and Engels argue that the tendencies attacked under this head misunderstand the nature of the communist movement. Instead of seeing it as springing from the needs and situation of a particular class, they wish to attain a more elevated tone by concerning themselves with the "most reasonable" social order, by revealing for the first time the absolute, "true" socialism.

[1] *The German Ideology*, pp. 311–16.

The authors ascribe this misunderstanding to the absence in Germany of any "real party conflict".

The first and last wisdom of this trend is the "demand" that society be made fit for "Man", that is, it must be adequate to "human nature". Marx and Engels criticise the abstract philosophical nature of this concept and insist on the necessity for studying real social relations, which would rapidly make apparent the large historical component in human nature.

A large part of this section consists of a tiresome detailed demonstration of the way "true" socialist writers know nothing of French and English communism directly, but merely plagiarise secondary sources.

Introduction to the Critique of Political Economy

This paper of 1857 is given here as an appendix and contains interesting remarks on bourgeois individualism, Greek art, and the relation of production to consumption and distribution. However, the most interesting section is perhaps the one on the method of political economy which is sure to play an increasingly larger part in discussion of this subject. One point Marx makes, to which I would like to draw attention, is that the order of categories used to correctly analyse a given system, e.g. capitalism, may be different from the order in which they appeared in history.

This raises also the whole issue of the relation between systemic and genetic analysis. It is one thing to say how the elements of a given structure condition one another: it is another thing to explain whence the elements arose and combined. Neglect of this distinction in Marxist theory may lead to technological determinism,[1] extrapolating unwisely from such Marxian dicta as "the handmill gives you society with the feudal lord, the steam-mill society with the industrial capitalist". In this example it should be understood that "gives" is not an historical category but a structural one about the social relations appropriate to a given productive force. The analysis of the *change* from a feudal to a capitalist mode of production is another question altogether. To treat such historical developments as though they were nothing but the passive reflection of an autonomous technological development is to fall into the most simplified and vulgar kind of evolutionism. Quite clearly, in the Marxist analysis of revolutionary

[1] For Lukacs on Bukharin's technological determinism see *New Left Review*, 39.

change, the essential point is that reference has to be made to class struggles, political conflicts, and ideological arguments. The revolution itself may well be the precondition of a subsequent flowering of technology.

University of Sussex, November 1969   C. J. ARTHUR

Karl Marx and Frederick Engels

THE GERMAN
IDEOLOGY

PREFACE

Hitherto men have constantly made up for themselves false conceptions about themselves, about what they are and what they ought to be. They have arranged their relationships according to their ideas of God, of normal man, etc. The phantoms of their brains have got out of their hands. They, the creators, have bowed down before their creations. Let us liberate them from the chimeras, the ideas, dogmas, imaginary beings under the yoke of which they are pining away. Let us revolt against the rule of thoughts. Let us teach men, says one, to exchange these imaginations for thoughts which correspond to the essence of man; says the second, to take up a critical attitude to them; says the third, to knock them out of their heads; and—existing reality will collapse.

These innocent and childlike fancies are the kernel of the modern Young-Hegelian philosophy, which not only is received by the German public with horror and awe, but is announced by our philosophic heroes with the solemn consciousness of its cataclysmic dangerousness and criminal ruthlessness. The first volume of the present publication has the aim of uncloaking these sheep, who take themselves and are taken for wolves; of showing how their bleating merely imitates in a philosophic form the conceptions of the German middle class; how the boasting of these philosophic commentators only mirrors the wretchedness of the real conditions in Germany. It is its aim to debunk and discredit the philosophic struggle with the shadows of reality, which appeals to the dreamy and muddled German nation.

Once upon a time a valiant fellow had the idea that men were drowned in water only because they were possessed with the idea of gravity. If they were to knock this notion out of their heads, say by stating it to be a superstition, a religious concept, they would be sublimely proof against any danger from water. His whole life long he fought against the illusion of gravity, of whose harmful results all statistics brought him new and manifold evidence. This honest fellow was the type of the new revolutionary philosophers in Germany.

I

FEUERBACH

OPPOSITION OF THE MATERIALIST AND IDEALIST OUTLOOK

A. IDEALISM AND MATERIALISM

The Illusions of German Ideology

As we hear from German ideologists, Germany has in the last few years gone through an unparalleled revolution. The decomposition of the Hegelian philosophy, which began with Strauss, has developed into a universal ferment into which all the "powers of the past" are swept. In the general chaos mighty empires have arisen only to meet with immediate doom, heroes have emerged momentarily only to be hurled back into obscurity by bolder and stronger rivals. It was a revolution beside which the French Revolution was child's play, a world struggle beside which the struggles of the Diadochi [successors of Alexander the Great] appear insignificant. Principles ousted one another, heroes of the mind overthrew each other with unheard-of rapidity, and in the three years 1842-45 more of the past was swept away in Germany than at other times in three centuries.

All this is supposed to have taken place in the realm of pure thought.

Certainly it is an interesting event we are dealing with: the putrescence of the absolute spirit. When the last spark of its life had failed, the various components of this *caput mortuum* began to decompose, entered into new combinations and formed new substances. The industrialists of philosophy, who till then had lived on the exploitation of the absolute spirit, now seized upon the new combinations. Each with all possible zeal set about retailing his apportioned share. This naturally gave rise to competition, which, to start with, was carried on in moderately staid bourgeois fashion. Later when the German market was glutted, and the commodity in spite of all efforts found no response in the world market, the business was spoiled in the usual German manner by fabricated and fictitious production, deterioration in quality, adulteration of the raw materials, falsification of labels, fictitious purchases, bill-jobbing and a credit system devoid of any real basis. The competition turned into a bitter struggle, which is now being extolled and interpreted to us as a revolution of world significance, the begetter of the most prodigious results and achievements.

If we wish to rate at its true value this philosophic charlatanry, which awakens even in the breast of the honest German citizen a glow of national pride, if we wish to bring out clearly the pettiness, the parochial narrowness of this whole Young-Hegelian movement and in particular the tragicomic contrast between the illusions of these heroes about their achievements and the actual achievements themselves, we must look at the whole spectacle from a standpoint beyond the frontiers of Germany.

German criticism has, right up to its latest efforts, never quitted the realm of philosophy. Far from examining its general philosophic premises, the whole body of its inquiries has actually sprung from the soil of a definite philosophical system, that of Hegel. Not only in their answers but in their very questions there was a mystification. This dependence on Hegel is the reason why not one of these modern critics has even attempted a comprehensive criticism of the Hegelian system, however much each professes to have advanced beyond Hegel. Their polemics against Hegel and against one another are confined to this—each extracts one side of the Hegelian system and turns this against the whole system as well as against the sides extracted by the others. To begin with they extracted pure unfalsified Hegelian categories such as "substance" and "self-consciousness", later they desecrated these categories with more secular names such as "species", "the Unique", "Man", etc.

The entire body of German philosophical criticism from Strauss to Stirner is confined to criticism of *religious* conceptions. The critics started from real religion and actual theology. What religious consciousness and a religious conception really meant was determined variously as they went along. Their advance consisted in subsuming the allegedly dominant metaphysical, political, juridical, moral and other conceptions under the class of religious or theological conceptions; and similarly in pronouncing political, juridical, moral consciousness as religious or theological, and the political, juridical, moral man— "*man*" in the last resort—as religious. The dominance of religion was taken for granted. Gradually every dominant relationship was pronounced a religious relationship and transformed into a cult, a cult of law, a cult of the State, etc. On all sides it was only a question of dogmas and belief in dogmas. The world sanctified to an ever-increasing extent till at last our venerable Saint Max was able to canonise it *en bloc* and thus dispose of it once for all.

The Old Hegelians had *comprehended* everything as soon as it was reduced to an Hegelian logical category. The Young Hegelians *criticised* everything by attributing to it religious conceptions or by pronouncing it a theological matter. The Young Hegelians are in agreement with the Old Hegelians in their belief in the rule of religion, of concepts, of a universal principle in the existing world. Only, the one party attacks this dominion as usurpation, while the other extols it as legitimate.

Since the Young Hegelians consider conceptions, thoughts, ideas, in fact all the products of consciousness, to which they attribute an independent existence, as the real chains of men (just as the Old Hegelians declared them the true bonds of human society) it is evident that the Young Hegelians have to fight only against these illusions of consciousness. Since, according to their fantasy, the relationships of men, all their doings, their chains and their limitations are products of their consciousness, the Young Hegelians logically put to men the moral postulate of exchanging their present consciousness for human, critical or egoistic consciousness, and thus of removing their limitations. This demand to change consciousness amounts to a demand to interpret reality in another way, i.e. to recognise it by means of another interpretation. The Young-Hegelian ideologists, in spite of their allegedly "world-shattering" statements, are the staunchest conservatives. The most recent of them have found the correct expression for their activity when they declare they are only fighting against "*phrases*". They forget, however, that to these phrases they themselves are only opposing other phrases, and that they are in no way combating the real existing world when they are merely combating the phrases of this world. The only results which this philosophic criticism could achieve were a few (and at that thoroughly one-sided) elucidations of Christianity from the point of view of religious history; all the rest of their assertions are only further embellishments of their claim to have furnished, in these unimportant elucidations, discoveries of universal importance.

It has not occurred to any one of these philosophers to inquire into the connection of German philosophy with German reality, the relation of their criticism to their own material surroundings.

First Premises of Materialist Method

The premises from which we begin are not arbitrary ones, not dogmas, but real premises from which abstraction can only be made in the imagination. They are the real individuals, their activity and the material conditions under which they live, both those which they find already existing and those produced by their activity. These premises can thus be verified in a purely empirical way.

The first premise of all human history is, of course, the existence of living human individuals. Thus the first fact to be established is the physical organisation of these individuals and their consequent relation to the rest of nature. Of course, we cannot here go either into the actual physical nature of man, or into the natural conditions in which man finds himself—geological, oreohydrographical, climatic and so on. The writing of history must always set out from these natural bases and their modification in the course of history through the action of men.

Men can be distinguished from animals by consciousness, by religion or anything else you like. They themselves begin to distinguish themselves from animals as soon as they begin to *produce* their means of subsistence, a step which is conditioned by their physical organisation. By producing their means of subsistence men are indirectly producing their actual material life.

The way in which men produce their means of subsistence depends first of all on the nature of the actual means of subsistence they find in existence and have to reproduce. This mode of production must not be considered simply as being the production of the physical existence of the individuals. Rather it is a definite form of activity of these individuals, a definite form of expressing their life, a definite *mode of life* on their part. As individuals express their life, so they are. What they are, therefore, coincides with their production, both with *what* they produce and with *how* they produce. The nature of individuals thus depends on the material conditions determining their production.

This production only makes its appearance with the *increase of population*. In its turn this presupposes the *intercourse [Verkehr]*[1] of

[1] In *The German Ideology* the word *"Verkehr"* is used in a very wide sense, encompassing the material and spiritual intercourse of separate individuals, social groups and entire countries. Marx and Engels show that material intercourse, and above all the intercourse of men with each other in the production process, is the basis of every other form of intercourse.

The terms *"Verkehrstorm"* (form of intercourse), *"Verkehrsweise"* (mode of intercourse) and *"Verkehrsverhaltnisse"* (relations, or conditions, of intercourse) which we encounter

individuals with one another. The form of this intercourse is again
determined by production.

The relations of different nations among themselves depend upon
the extent to which each has developed its productive forces, the
division of labour and internal intercourse. This statement is generally
recognised. But not only the relation of one nation to others, but also
the whole internal structure of the nation itself depends on the stage
of development reached by its production and its internal and external
intercourse. How far the productive forces of a nation are developed
is shown most manifestly by the degree to which the division of
labour has been carried. Each new productive force, insofar as it is
not merely a quantitative extension of productive forces already known
(for instance the bringing into cultivation of fresh land), causes a
further development of the division of labour.

The division of labour inside a nation leads at first to the separation
of industrial and commercial from agricultural labour, and hence to the
separation of *town* and *country* and to the conflict of their interests. Its
further development leads to the separation of commerical from
industrial labour. At the same time through the division of labour
inside these various branches there develop various divisions among the
individuals co-operating in definite kinds of labour. The relative
position of these individual groups is determined by the methods
employed in agriculture, industry and commerce (patriarchalism,
slavery, estates, classes). These same conditions are to be seen (given
a more developed intercourse) in the relations of different nations to
one another.

The various stages of development in the division of labour are
just so many different forms of ownership, i.e. the existing stage in
the division of labour determines also the relations of individuals to
one another with reference to the material, instrument, and product
of labour.

The first form of ownership is tribal [*Stammeigentum*][1] ownership.

in *The German Ideology* are used by Marx and Engels to express the concept "relations of
production" which during that period was taking shape in their mind.

The ordinary dictionary meanings of *"Verkehr"* are traffic, intercourse, commerce.
In this translation the word *"Verkehr"* has been mostly rendered as "intercourse" and
occasionally as "association" or "commerce".—Ed.

[1] The term *"Stamm"*—rendered in the present volume by the word "tribe"—played
a considerably greater part in historical works written during the forties of the last
century than it does at present. It was used to denote a community of people descended
from a common ancestor, and comprised the modern concepts of "gens" and "tribe".
The first to define and differentiate these concepts was Lewis Henry Morgan in his work

It corresponds to the undeveloped stage of production, at which a people lives by hunting and fishing, by the rearing of beasts or, in the highest stage, agriculture. In the latter case it presupposes a great mass of uncultivated stretches of land. The division of labour is at this stage still very elementary and is confined to a further extension of the natural division of labour existing in the family. The social structure is, therefore, limited to an extension of the family; patriarchal family chieftains, below them the members of the tribe, finally slaves. The slavery latent in the family only develops gradually with the increase of population, the growth of wants, and with the extension of external relations, both of war and of barter.

The second form is the ancient communal and State ownership which proceeds especially from the union of several tribes into a *city* by agreement or by conquest, and which is still accompanied by slavery. Beside communal ownership we already find movable, and later also immovable, private property developing, but as an abnormal form subordinate to communal ownership. The citizens hold power over their labouring slaves only in their community, and on this account alone, therefore, they are bound to the form of communal ownership. It is the communal private property which compels the active citizens to remain in this spontaneously derived form of association over against their slaves. For this reason the whole structure of society based on this communal ownership, and with it the power of the people, decays in the same measure as, in particular, immovable private property evolves. The division of labour is already more developed. We already find the antagonism of town and country; later the antagonism between those states which represent town interests and those which represent country interests, and inside the towns themselves the antagonism between industry and maritime commerce. The class relation between citizens and slaves is now completely developed.

With the development of private property, we find here for the first time the same conditions which we shall find again, only on a more extensive scale, with modern private property. On the one hand,

Ancient Society; or, Researches in the Lines of Human Progress from Savagery Through Barbarism to Civilisation, London, 1877. This outstanding American ethnographer and historian showed for the first time the significance of the gens as the nucleus of the primitive communal system and thereby laid the scientific foundations for the history of primitive society as a whole. Engels drew the general conclusions from Morgan's discoveries and made a comprehensive analysis of the meaning of the concepts "gens" and "tribe" in his work *The Origin of the Family, Private Property and the State* (1884).—Ed.

the concentration of private property, which began very early in Rome (as the Licinian agrarian law proves[1]) and proceeded very rapidly from the time of the civil wars and especially under the Emperors; on the other hand, coupled with this, the transformation of the plebeian small peasantry into a proletariat, which, however, owing to its intermediate position between propertied citizens and slaves, never achieved an independent development.

The third form of ownership is feudal or estate property. If antiquity started out from the *town* and its little territory, the Middle Ages started out from the *country*. This different starting-point was determined by the sparseness of the population at that time, which was scattered over a large area and which received no large increase from the conquerors. In contrast to Greece and Rome, feudal development at the outset, therefore, extends over a much wider territory, prepared by the Roman conquests and the spread of agriculture at first associated with it. The last centuries of the declining Roman Empire and its conquest by the barbarians destroyed a number of productive forces; agriculture had declined, industry had decayed for want of a market, trade had died out or been violently suspended, the rural and urban population had decreased. From these conditions and the mode of organisation of the conquest determined by them, feudal property developed under the influence of the Germanic military constitution. Like tribal and communal ownership, it is based again on a community; but the directly producing class standing over against it is not, as in the case of the ancient community, the slaves, but the enserfed small peasantry. As soon as feudalism is fully developed, there also arises antagonism to the towns. The hierarchical structure of landownership, and the armed bodies of retainers associated with it, gave the nobility power over the serfs. This feudal organisation was, just as much as the ancient communal ownership, an association against a subjected producing class; but the form of association and the relation to the direct producers were different because of the different conditions of production.

This feudal system of landownership had its counterpart in the *towns* in the shape of corporative property, the feudal organisation of trades. Here property consisted chiefly in the labour of each individual

[1] The *Licinian agrarian law*—the agrarian law of Licinius and Sextius, Roman tribunes of the people, passed in 367 B.C. as a result of the struggle which the plebeians waged against the patricians. According to this law a Roman citizen could not hold more than 500 Yugera (approximately 309 acres) of common land (*ager publicus*).—Ed.

person. The necessity for association against the organised robber-nobility, the need for communal covered markets in an age when the industrialist was at the same time a merchant, the growing competition of the escaped serfs swarming into the rising towns, the feudal structure of the whole country: these combined to bring about the *guilds*. The gradually accumulated small capital of individual craftsmen and their stable numbers, as against the growing population, evolved the relation of journeyman and apprentice, which brought into being in the towns a hierarchy similar to that in the country.

Thus the chief form of property during the feudal epoch consisted on the one hand of landed property with serf labour chained to it, and on the other of the labour of the individual with small capital commanding the labour of journeymen. The organisation of both was determined by the restricted conditions of production—the small-scale and primitive cultivation of the land, and the craft type of industry. There was little division of labour in the heyday of feudalism. Each country bore in itself the antithesis of town and country; the division into estates was certainly strongly marked; but apart from the differentiation of princes, nobility, clergy and peasants in the country, and masters, journeymen, apprentices and soon also the rabble of casual labourers in the towns, no division of importance took place. In agriculture it was rendered difficult by the strip-system, beside which the cottage industry of the peasants themselves emerged. In industry there was no division of labour at all in the individual trades themselves, and very little between them. The separation of industry and commerce was found already in existence in older towns; in the newer it only developed later, when the towns entered into mutual relations.

The grouping of larger territories into feudal kingdoms was a necessity for the landed nobility as for the towns. The organisation of the ruling class, the nobility, had, therefore, everywhere a monarch at its head.

The fact is, therefore, that definite individuals who are productively active in a definite way enter into these definite social and political relations. Empirical observation must in each separate instance bring out empirically, and without any mystification and speculation, the connection of the social and political structure with production. The social structure and the State are continually evolving out of the life-process of definite individuals, but of individuals, not as they may appear in their own or other people's imagination, but as they *really* are; i.e. as they operate, produce materially, and hence as they work under definite material limits, presuppositions and conditions independent of their will.

The production of ideas, of conceptions, of consciousness, is at first directly interwoven with the material activity and the material intercourse of men, the language of real life. Conceiving, thinking, the mental intercourse of men, appear at this stage as the direct efflux of their material behaviour. The same applies to mental production as expressed in the language of politics, laws, morality, religion, metaphysics, etc. of a people. Men are the producers of their conceptions, ideas, etc.—real, active men, as they are conditioned by a definite development of their productive forces and of the intercourse corresponding to these, up to its furthest forms. Consciousness can never be anything else than conscious existence, and the existence of men is their actual life-process. If in all ideology men and their circumstances appear upside-down as in a *camera obscura*, this phenomenon arises just as much from their historical life-process as the inversion of objects on the retina does from their physical life-process.

In direct contrast to German philosophy which descends from heaven to earth, here we ascend from earth to heaven. That is to say, we do not set out from what men say, imagine, conceive, nor from men as narrated, thought of, imagined, conceived, in order to arrive at men in the flesh. We set out from real, active men, and on the basis of their real life-process we demonstrate the development of the ideological reflexes and echoes of this life-process. The phantoms formed in the human brain are also, necessarily, sublimates of their material life-process, which is empirically verifiable and bound to material premises. Morality, religion, metaphysics, all the rest of ideology and their corresponding forms of consciousness, thus no longer retain the semblance of independence. They have no history, no development; but men, developing their material production and their material intercourse, alter, along with this their real existence, their thinking and the products of their thinking. Life is not determined by conciousness, but consciousness by life. In the first method of approach the starting-point is consciousness taken as the living individual; in the second method, which conforms to real life, it is the real living individuals themselves, and consciousness is considered solely as *their* consciousness.

This method of approach is not devoid of premises. It starts out from the real premises and does not abandon them for a moment. Its premises are men, not in any fantastic isolation and rigidity, but in their actual, empirically perceptible process of development under definite conditions. As soon as this active life-process is described, history ceases to be a collection of dead facts as it is with the empiricists (themselves still abstract), or an imagined activity of imagined subjects, as with the idealists.

Where speculation ends—in real life—there real, positive science begins: the representation of the practical activity, of the practical process of development of men. Empty talk about consciousness ceases, and real knowledge has to take its place. When reality is depicted, philosophy as an independent branch of knowledge loses its medium of existence. At the best its place can only be taken by a summing-up of the most general results, abstractions which arise from the observation of the historical development of men. Viewed apart from real history, these abstractions have in themselves no value whatsoever. They can only serve to facilitate the arrangement of historical material, to indicate the sequence of its separate strata. But they by no means afford a recipe or schema, as does philosophy, for neatly trimming the epochs of history. On the contrary, our difficulties begin only when we set about the observation and the arrangement—the real depiction—of our historical material, whether of a past epoch or of the present. The removal of these difficulties is governed by premises which it is quite impossible to state here, but which only the study of the actual life-process and the activity of the individuals of each epoch will make evident. We shall select here some of these abstractions, which we use in contradistinction to the ideologists, and shall illustrate them by historical examples.

History: Fundamental Conditions

Since we are dealing with the Germans, who are devoid of premises, we must begin by stating the first premise of all human existence and, therefore, of all history, the premise, namely, that men must be in a position to live in order to be able to "make history". But life involves before everything else eating and drinking, a habitation, clothing and many other things. The first historical act is thus the production of the means to satisfy these needs, the production of material life itself. And indeed this is an historical act, a fundamental condition of all history, which today, as thousands of years ago, must daily and hourly be fulfilled merely in order to sustain human life. Even when the sensuous world is reduced to a minimum, to a stick as with Saint Bruno [Bauer], it presupposes the action of producing the stick.

Therefore in any interpretation of history one has first of all to observe this fundamental fact in all its significance and all its implications and to accord it its due importance. It is well known that the Germans have never done this, and they have never, therefore, had an *earthly* basis for history and consequently never an historian. The French and the English, even if they have conceived the relation of this fact with so-called history only in an extremely one-sided fashion, particularly as long as they remained in the toils of political ideology, have nevertheless made the first attempts to give the writing of history a materialistic basis by being the first to write histories of civil society, of commerce and industry.

The second point is that the satisfaction of the first need (the action of satisfying, and the instrument of satisfaction which has been acquired) leads to new needs; and this production of new needs is the first historical act. Here we recognise immediately the spiritual ancestry of the great historical wisdom of the Germans who, when they run out of positive material and when they can serve up neither theological nor political nor literary rubbish, assert that this is not history at all, but the "prehistoric era". They do not, however, enlighten us as to how we proceed from this nonsensical "prehistory" to history proper; although, on the other hand, in their historical speculation they seize upon this "prehistory" with especial eagerness because they imagine themselves safe there from interference on the part of "crude facts", and, at the same time, because there they can give full rein to their speculative impulse and set up and knock down hypotheses by the thousand.

The third circumstance which, from the very outset, enters into historical development, is that men, who daily remake their own life, begin to make other men, to propagate their kind: the relation between man and woman, parents and children, the *family*. The family, which to begin with is the only social relationship, becomes later, when increased needs create a new social relations and the increased population new needs, a subordinate one (except in Germany), and must then be treated and analysed according to the existing empirical data, not according to "the concept of the family", as is the custom in Germany.[1]

---

[1] The building of houses. With savages each family has as a matter of course its own cave or hut like the separate family tent of the nomads. This separate domestic economy is made only the more necessary by the further development of private property. With the agricultural peoples a communal domestic economy is just as impossible as a communal cultivation of the soil. A great advance was the building of towns. In all previous periods, however, the abolition of individual economy, which is inseparable from the abolition of private property, was impossible for the simple reason that the material conditions

These three aspects of social activity are not of course to be taken as three different stages, but just as three aspects or, to make it clear to the Germans, three "moments", which have existed simultaneously since the dawn of history and the first men, and which still assert themselves in history today.

The production of life, both of one's own in labour and of fresh life in procreation, now appears as a double relationship: on the one hand as a natural, on the other as a social relationship. By social we understand the co-operation of several individuals, no matter under what conditions, in what manner and to what end. It follows from this that a certain mode of production, or industrial stage, is always combined with a certain mode of co-operation, or social stage, and this mode of co-operation is itself a "productive force". Further, that the multitude of productive forces accessible to men determines the nature of society, hence, that the "history of humanity" must always be studied and treated in relation to the history of industry and exchange. But it is also clear how in Germany it is impossible to write this sort of history, because the Germans lack not only the necessary power of comprehension and the material but also the "evidence of their senses", for across the Rhine you cannot have any experience of these things since history has stopped happening. Thus it is quite obvious from the start that there exists a materialistic connection of men with one another, which is determined by their needs and their mode of production, and which is as old as men themselves. This connection is ever taking on new forms, and thus presents a "history" independently of the existence of any political or religious nonsense which in addition may hold men together.

Only now, after having considered four moments, four aspects of the primary historical relationships, do we find that man also possesses "consciousness", but, even so, not inherent, not "pure" consciousness. From the start the "spirit" is afflicted with the curse of being "burdened" with matter, which here makes its appearance in the form of

governing it were not present. The setting-up of a communal domestic economy presupposes the development of machinery, of the use of natural forces and of many other productive forces—e.g. of water-supplies, of gas-lighting, steam-heating, etc., the removal [of the antagonism] of town and country. Without these conditions a communal economy would not in itself form a new productive force; lacking any material basis and resting on a purely theoretical foundation, it would be a mere freak and would end in nothing more than a monastic economy—What was possible can be seen in the towns brought about by condensation and the erection of communal buildings for various definite purposes (prisons, barracks, etc.). That the abolition of individual economy is inseparable from the abolition of the family is self-evident.

agitated layers of air, sounds, in short, of language. Language is as old as consciousness, language *is* practical consciousness that exists also for other men, and for that reason alone it really exists for me personally as well; language, like consciousness, only arises from the need, the necessity, of intercourse with other men. Where there exists a relationship, it exists for me: the animal does not enter into *"relations"* with anything, it does not enter into any relation at all. For the animal, its relation to others does not exist as a relation. Consciousness is, therefore, from the very beginning a social product, and remains so as long as men exist at all. Consciousness is at first, of course, merely consciouness concerning the *immediate* sensuous environment and consciousness of the limited connection with other persons and things outside the individual who is growing self-conscious. At the same time it is consciousness of nature, which first appears to men as a completely alien, all-powerful and unassailable force, with which men's relations are purely animal and by which they are overawed like beasts; it is thus a purely animal consciousness of nature (natural religion) just because nature is as yet hardly modified historically. (We see here immediately: this natural religion or this particular relation of men to nature is determined by the form of society and vice versa. Here, as everywhere, the identity of nature and man appears in such a way that the restricted relation of men to nature determines their restricted relation to one another, and their restricted relation to one another determines men's restricted relation to nature.) On the other hand, man's consciousness of the necessity of associating with the individuals around him is the beginning of the consciousness that he is living in society at all. This beginning is as animal as social life itself at this stage. It is mere herd-consciousness, and at this point man is only distinguished from sheep by the fact that with him consciousness takes the place of instinct or that his instinct is a conscious one. This sheep-like or tribal consciousness receives its further development and extension through increased productivity, the increase of needs, and, what is fundamental to both of these, the increase of population. With these there develops the division of labour, which was originally nothing but the division of labour in the sexual act, then that division of labour which develops spontaneously or "naturally" by virtue of natural predisposition (e.g. physical strength), needs, accidents, etc. etc. Division of labour only becomes truly such from the moment when a division of material and mental labour appears. (The first form of ideologists, *priests*, is concurrent.) From this moment onwards consciousness *can* really flatter itself that it is something other than consciousness of existing practice, that it *really* represents something without representing something real; from now on consciousness is in a position to emancipate itself from the world and to proceed to the formation of "pure" theory, theology, philosophy, ethics, etc. But even if this theory, theology, philosophy, ethics, etc. comes into contradiction with the existing relations, this can only occur because existing social relations have come into contradiction with existing forces of production; this, moreover, can also occur in a particular national sphere of relations through the appearance of the contradiction, not within the national orbit, but between this national consciousness and the practice of other nations, i.e. between the national and the general consciousness of a nation (as we see it now in Germany).

Moreover, it is quite immaterial what consciousness starts to do on its own: out of all such muck we get only the one inference that these three moments, the forces of production, the state of society, and consciousness, can and must come into contradiction with one another, because the *division of labour* implies the possibility, nay the fact that intellectual and material activity—enjoyment and labour, production and consumption—devolve on different individuals, and that the only possibility of their not coming into contradiction lies in the negation in its turn of the division of labour. It is self-evident, moreover, that "spectres", "bonds", "the higher being", "concept", "scruple", are merely the idealistic, spiritual expression, the conception apparently of the isolated individual, the image of very empirical fetters and limitations, within which the mode of production of life and the form of intercourse coupled with it move.

Private Property and Communism

With the division of labour, in which all these contradictions are implicit, and which in its turn is based on the natural division of labour in the family and the separation of society into individual families opposed to one another, is given simultaneously the *distribution*, and indeed the *unequal* distribution, both quantitative and qualitative, of labour and its products, hence property: the nucleus, the first form, of which lies in the family, where wife and children are the slaves of the husband. This latent slavery in the family, though still very crude, is the first property, but even at this early stage it corresponds perfectly to the definition of modern economists who call it the power of disposing of the labour-power of others. Division of labour and private property are, moreover, identical expressions: in the one the same thing is affirmed with reference to activity as is affirmed in the other with reference to the product of the activity.

Further, the division of labour implies the contradiction between the interest of the separate individual or the individual family and the communal interest of all individuals who have intercourse with one another. And indeed, this communal interest does not exist merely in the imagination, as the "general interest", but first of all in reality, as the mutual interdependence of the individuals among whom the labour is divided. And finally, the division of labour offers us the first example of how, as long as man remains in natural society, that is, as long as a cleavage exists between the particular and the common interest, as long, therefore, as activity is not voluntarily, but naturally, divided, man's own deed becomes an alien power opposed to him, which enslaves him instead of being controlled by him. For as soon as the distribution of labour comes into being, each man has a particular, exclusive sphere of activity, which is forced upon him and from which he cannot escape. He is a hunter, a fisherman, a shepherd, or a critical critic, and must remain so if he does not want to lose his means of livelihood; while in communist society, where nobody has one exclusive sphere of activity but each can become accomplished in any branch he wishes, society regulates the general production and thus makes it possible for me to do one thing today and another tomorrow, to hunt in the morning, fish in the afternoon, rear cattle in the evening, criticise after dinner, just as I have a mind, without ever becoming hunter, fisherman, shepherd or critic. This fixation of social activity, this consolidation of what we ourselves produce into an objective power above us, growing out of our control, thwarting our expectations, bringing to naught our calculations, is one of the chief factors in historical development up till now.

[1] (And out of this very contradiction between the interest of the individual and that of the community the latter takes an independent form as the *State*, divorced from the real interests of individual and community, and at the same time as an illusory communal life, always based, however, on the real ties existing in every family and tribal conglomeration—such as flesh and blood, language, division of labour on a larger scale, and other interests—and especially, as we shall

---

[1] In the manuscript this paragraph occurs as a marginal note beside the previous paragraph.—Ed.

enlarge upon later, on the classes, already determined by the division of labour, which in every such mass of men separate out, and of which one dominates all the others. It follows from this that all struggles within the State, the struggle between democracy, aristocracy, and monarchy, the struggle for the franchise, etc. etc. are merely the illusory forms in which the real struggles of the different classes are fought out among one another. Of this the German theoreticians have not the faintest inkling, although they have received a sufficient introduction to the subject in the *Deutsch-Französische Jahrbücher* and *Die heilige Familie*. Further, it follows that every class which is struggling for mastery, even when its domination, as is the case with the proletariat, postulates the abolition of the old form of society in its entirety and of domination itself, must first conquer for itself political power in order to represent its interest in turn as the general interest, which immediately it is forced to do. Just because individuals seek *only* their particular interest, which for them does not coincide with their communal interest, the latter will be imposed on them as an interest "alien" to them, and "independent" of them, as in its turn a particular, peculiar "general" interest; or they themselves must remain within this discord, as in democracy. On the other hand, too, the *practical* struggle of these particular interests, which constantly *really* run counter to the communal and illusory communal interests, makes *practical* intervention and control necessary through the illusory "general" interest in the form of the State.)

The social power, i.e. the multiplied productive force, which arises through the co-operation of different individuals as it is determined by the division of labour, appears to these individuals, since their co-operation is not voluntary but has come about naturally, not as their own united power, but as an alien force existing outside them, of the origin and goal of which they are ignorant, which they thus cannot control, which on the contrary passes through a peculiar series of phases and stages independent of the will and the action of man, nay even being the prime governor of these.

How otherwise could for instance property have had a history at all, have taken on different forms, and landed property, for example, according to the different premises given, have proceeded in France from parcellation to centralisation in the hands of a few, in England from centralisation in the hands of a few to parcellation, as is actually the case today? Or how does it happen that trade, which after all is nothing more than the exchange of products of various individuals and countries, rules the whole world through the relation of supply and demand—a relation which, as an English economist says, hovers over the earth like the fate of the ancients, and with invisible hand allots fortune and misfortune to men, sets up empires and overthrows empires, causes nations to rise and to disappear—while with the abolition of the basis of private property, with the communistic regulation of production (and, implicit in this, the destruction of the alien relation between men and what they themselves produce), the power of the relation of supply and demand is dissolved into nothing, and men get exchange, production, the mode of their mutual relation, under their own control again?

In history up to the present it is certainly an empirical fact that separate individuals have, with the broadening of their activity into world-historical activity, become more and more enslaved under a power alien to them (a pressure which they have conceived of as a dirty trick on the part of the so-called universal spirit, etc.), a power which has become more and more enormous and, in the last instance, turns out to be the *world market*. But it is just as empirically established that, by the overthrow of the existing state of society by the communist revolution (of which more below) and the abolition of private property which is identical with it, this power, which so baffles the German theoreticians, will be dissolved; and that then the liberation of each single individual will be accomplished in the measure in which history becomes transformed into world history. From the above it is clear that the real intellectual wealth of the individual depends entirely on the wealth of his real connections. Only then will the separate individuals be liberated from the various national and local barriers, be brought into practical connection with the material and intellectual production of the whole world and be put in a position to acquire the capacity to enjoy this all-sided production of the whole earth (the creations of man). *All-round* dependence, this natural form of the *world-historical* co-operation of individuals, will be transformed by this communist revolution into the control and conscious mastery of these powers, which, born of the action of men on one another, have till now overawed and governed men as powers completely alien to them. Now this view can be expressed again in speculative-idealistic, i.e. fantastic, terms as "self-generation of the species" ("society as the subject"), and thereby the consecutive series of interrelated individuals connected with each other can be conceived as a single individual, which accomplishes the mystery of generating itself. It is clear here that individuals certainly make *one another*, physically and mentally, but do not make themselves.

This "alienation" (to use a term which will be comprehensible to the philosophers) can, of course, only be abolished given two *practical* premises. For it to become an "intolerable" power, i.e. a power against which men make a revolution, it must necessarily have rendered the great mass of humanity "propertyless", and produced, at the same time, the contradiction of an existing world of wealth and culture, both of which conditions presuppose a great increase in productive power, a high degree of its development. And, on the other hand, this development of productive forces (which itself implies the actual empirical existence of men in their *world-historical*, instead of local, being) is an absolutely necessary practical premise because without it *want* is merely made general, and with *destitution* the struggle for necessities and all the old filthy business would necessarily be reproduced; and furthermore, because only with this universal development of productive forces is a *universal* intercourse between men established, which produces in all nations simultaneously the phenomenon of the "propertyless" mass (universal competition), makes each nation dependent on the revolutions of the others, and finally has put *world-historical*, empirically universal individuals in place of local ones. Without this, (1) communism could only exist as a local event; (2) the *forces* of intercourse themselves could not have developed as *universal*, hence intolerable powers: they would have remained home-bred conditions surrounded by superstition; and (3) each extension of intercourse would abolish local communism. Empirically, communism is only possible as the act of the dominant peoples "all at once" and simultaneously, which presupposes the universal development of productive forces and the world intercourse bound up with communism. Moreover, the mass of *propertyless* workers—the utterly precarious position of labour-power on a mass scale cut off from capital or from even a limited satisfaction and, therefore, no longer merely temporarily deprived of work itself as a secure source of life—presupposes the *world market* through competition. The proletariat can thus only exist *world-historically*, just as communism, its activity, can only have a "world-historical" existence. World-historical existence of individuals means, existence of individuals which is directly linked up with world history.

Communism is for us not a *state of affairs* which is to be established, an *ideal* to which reality [will] have to adjust itself. We call communism the *real* movement which abolishes the present state of things. The conditions of this movement result from the premises now in existence.

Civil Society and the Conception of History

The form of intercourse determined by the existing productive forces at all previous historical stages, and in its turn determining these, is *civil society*. The latter, as is clear from what we have said above, has as its premises and basis the simple family and the multiple, the so-called tribe, the more precise determinants of this society are enumerated in our remarks above. Already here we see how this civil society is the true source and theatre of all history, and how absurd is the conception of history held hitherto, which neglects the real relationships and confines itself to high-sounding dramas of princes and states.

Civil society embraces the whole material intercourse of individuals within a definite stage of the development of productive forces. It embraces the whole commercial and industrial life of a given stage and, insofar, transcends the State and the nation, though, on the other hand again, it must assert itself in its foreign relations as nationality, and inwardly must organise itself as State. The word "civil" society [*bürgerliche Gesellschaft*] emerged in the eighteenth century, when property relationships had already extricated themselves from the ancient and medieval communal society. Civil society as such only develops with the bourgeoisie; the social organisation evolving directly out of production and commerce, which in all ages forms the basis of the State and of the rest of the idealistic superstructure, has, however, always been designated by the same name.

History is nothing but the succession of the separate generations, each of which exploits the materials, the capital funds, the productive forces handed down to it by all preceding generations, and thus, on the one hand, continues the traditional activity in completely changed circumstances and, on the other, modifies the old circumstances with a completely changed activity. This can be speculatively distorted so that later history is made the goal of earlier history, e.g. the goal ascribed to the discovery of America is to further the eruption of the French Revolution. Thereby history receives its own special aims and becomes "a person ranking with other persons" (to wit: "Self-Consciousness, Criticism, the Unique", etc.), while what is designated with the words "destiny", "goal", "germ", or "idea" of earlier history is nothing more than an abstraction formed from later history, from the active influence which earlier history exercises on later history.

The further the separate spheres, which interact on one another, extend in the course of this development, the more the original isolation of the separate nationalities is destroyed by the developed mode of production and intercourse and the division of labour between various nations naturally brought forth by these, the more history becomes world history. Thus, for instance, if in England a machine is invented, which deprives countless workers of bread in India and China, and overturns the whole form of existence of these empires, this invention becomes a world-historical fact. Or again, take the case of sugar and coffee which have proved their world-historical importance in the nineteenth century by the fact that the lack of these products, occasioned by the Napoleonic Continental System, caused the Germans to rise against Napoleon, and thus became the real basis of the glorious Wars of liberation of 1813. From this it follows that this transformation of history into world history is not indeed a mere abstract act on the part of the "self-consciousness", the world spirit, or of any other metaphysical spectre, but a quite material, empirically verifiable act, an act the proof of which every individual furnishes as he comes and goes, eats, drinks and clothes himself.

This conception of history depends on our ability to expound the real process of production, starting out from the material production of life itself, and to comprehend the form of intercourse connected with this and created by this mode of production (i.e. civil society in its various stages), as the basis of all history; and to show it in its action as State, to explain all the different theoretical products and forms of consciousness, religion, philosophy, ethics, etc. etc. and trace their origins and growth from that basis; by which means, of course, the whole thing can be depicted in its totality (and therefore, too, the reciprocal action of these various sides on one another). It has not, like the idealistic view of history, in every period to look for a category, but remains constantly on the real *ground* of history; it does not explain practice from the idea but explains the formation of ideas from material practice; and accordingly it comes to the conclusion that all forms and products of consciousness cannot be dissolved by mental criticism, by resolution into "self-consciousness" or transformation into "apparitions", "spectres", "fancies", etc. but only by the practical overthrow of the actual social relations which gave rise to this idealistic humbug; that not criticism but revolution is the driving force of history, also of religion, of philosophy and all other types of theory. It shows that history does not end by being resolved into "self-consciousness" as "spirit of the spirit", but that in it at each stage there is found a material result: a sum of productive forces, an historically created relation of individuals to nature and to one another, which is handed down to each generation from its predecessor; a mass of productive forces, capital funds and conditions, which, on the one hand, is indeed modified by the new generation, but also on the other prescribes for it its conditions of life and gives it a definite development, a special character. It shows that circumstances make men just as much as men make circumstances.

This sum of productive forces, capital funds and social forms of intercourse, which every individual and generation finds in existence as something given, is the real basis of what the philosophers have conceived as "substance" and "essence of man", and what they have deified and attacked; a real basis which is not in the least disturbed, in its effect and influence on the development of men, by the fact that these philosophers revolt against it as "self-consciousness" and the "Unique". These conditions of life, which different generations find in existence, decide also whether or not the periodically recurring revolutionary convulsion will be strong enough to overthrow the basis of the entire existing system. And if these material elements of a complete revolution are not present (namely, on the one hand the existing productive forces, on the other the formation of a revolutionary mass, which revolts not only against separate conditions of society up till then, but against the very "production of life" till then, the "total activity" on which it was based), then, as far as practical development is concerned, it is absolutely immaterial whether the *idea* of this revolution has been expressed a hundred times already, as the history of communism proves.

In the whole conception of history up to the present this real basis of history has either been totally neglected or else considered as a minor matter quite irrelevant to the course of history. History must, therefore, always be written according to an extraneous standard; the real production of life seems to be primeval history, while the truly historical appears to be separated from ordinary life, something extra-superterrestrial. With this the relation of man to nature is excluded from history and hence the antithesis of nature and history is created. The exponents of this conception of history have consequently only been able to see in history the political actions of princes and States, religious and all sorts of theoretical struggles, and in particular in each historical epoch have had to *share the illusion of that epoch*. For instance, if an epoch imagines itself to be actuated by purely "political" or "religious" motives, although "religion" and "politics" are only forms of its true motives, the historian accepts this opinion. The "idea", the "conception" of the people in question about their real practice, is transformed into the sole determining, active force, which controls and determines their practice. When the crude form in which the division of labour appears with the Indians and Egyptians calls forth the caste-system in their State and religion, the historian believes that the caste-system is the power which has produced this crude social form. While the French and the English at least hold by the political illusion, which is moderately close to reality, the Germans move in the realm of the "pure spirit", and make religious illusion the driving force of history. The Hegelian philosophy of history is the last consequence, reduced to its "finest expression", of all this German historiography, for which it is not a question of real, nor even of political, interests, but of pure thoughts, which consequently must appear to Saint Bruno as a series of "thoughts" that devour one another and are finally swallowed up in "self-consciousness".

[1] (So-called *objective* historiography just consists in treating the historical conditions independent of activity. Reactionary character.)

Feuerbach: Philosophic, and Real, Liberation

[. . . .] It is also clear from these arguments how grossly Feuerbach is deceiving himself when (*Wigand's Vierteljahrsschrift*, 1845, Band 2) by virtue of the qualification "common man" he declares himself a communist, transforms the latter into a predicate of "man", and thereby thinks it possible to change the word "communist", which in the real world means the follower of a definite revolutionary party, into a mere category. Feuerbach's whole deduction with regard to the relation of men to one another goes only so far as to prove that men need and *always have needed* each other. He wants to establish consciousness of this fact, that is to say, like the other theorists, merely to produce a correct consciousness about an *existing* fact; whereas for the real communist it is a question of overthrowing the existing state of things. We thoroughly appreciate, moreover, that Feuerbach, in

[1] Marginal note by Marx—Ed.

endeavouring to produce consciousness of just *this* fact, is going as far as a theorist possibly can, without ceasing to be a theorist and philosopher. . . .

As an example of Feuerbach's acceptance and at the same time misunderstanding of existing reality, which he still shares with our opponents, we recall the passage in the *Philosophie der Zukunft* where he develops the view that the existence of a thing or a man is at the same time its or his essence, that the conditions of existence, the mode of life and activity of an animal or human individual are those in which its "essence" feels itself satisfied. Here every exception is expressly conceived as an unhappy chance, as an abnormality which cannot be altered. Thus if millions of proletarians feel by no means contented with their living conditions, if their "existence" does not in the least correspond to their "essence", then, according to the passage quoted, this is an unavoidable misfortune, which must be borne quietly. The millions of proletarians and communists, however, think differently and will prove this in time, when they bring their "existence" into harmony with their "essence" in a practical way, by means of a revolution. Feuerbach, therefore, never speaks of the world of man in such cases, but always takes refuge in external nature, and moreover in *nature* which has not yet been subdued by men. But every new invention, every advance made by industry, detaches another piece from this domain, so that the ground which produces examples illustrating such Feuerbachian propositions is steadily shrinking.

[. . . .] We shall, of course, not take the trouble to enlighten our wise philosophers by explaining to them that the "liberation" of "man" is not advanced a single step by reducing philosophy, theology, substance and all the trash to "self-consciousness" and by liberating man from the domination of these phrases, which have never held him in thrall. Nor will we explain to them that it is only possible to achieve real liberation in the real world and by employing real means, that slavery cannot be abolished without the steam-engine and the mule and spinning-jenny, serfdom cannot be abolished without improved agriculture, and that, in general, people cannot be liberated as long as they are unable to obtain food and drink, housing and clothing in adequate quality and quantity. "Liberation" is an historical and not a mental act, and it is brought about by historical conditions, the development of industry, commerce, agriculture, the conditions of intercourse. . . .[1]

---

[1] A gap in the manuscript.—*Ed.*

In Germany, a country where only a trivial historical development is taking place, these mental developments, these glorified and ineffective trivialities, naturally serve as a substitute for the lack of historical development, and they take root and have to be combated. But this fight is of local importance. . . .

In reality and for the *practical* materialist, i.e. the *communist*, it is a question of revolutionising the existing world, of practically attacking and changing existing things. When occasionally we find such views with Feuerbach, they are never more than isolated surmises and have much too little influence on his general outlook to be considered here as anything else than embryos capable of development. Feuerbach's "conception" of the sensuous world is confined on the one hand to mere contemplation of it, and on the other to mere feeling; he says "Man" instead of "real historical man". "Man" is really "the German". In the first case, the *contemplation* of the sensuous world, he necessarily lights on things which contradict his consciousness and feeling, which disturb the harmony he presupposes, the harmony of all parts of the sensuous world and especially of man and nature. To remove this disturbance, he must take refuge in a double perception, a profane one which only perceives the "flatly obvious" and a higher, philosophical, one which perceives the "true essence" of things. He does not see how the sensuous world around him is, not a thing given direct from all eternity, remaining ever the same, but the product of industry and of the state of society; and, indeed, in the sense that it is an historical product, the result of the activity of a whole succession of generations, each standing on the shoulders of the preceding one, developing its industry and its intercourse, modifying its social system according to the changed needs. Even the objects of the simplest "sensuous certainty" are only given him through social development, industry and commercial intercourse. The cherry-tree, like almost all fruit-trees, was, as is well known, only a few centuries ago transplanted by *commerce* into our zone, and therefore only *by* this action of a definite society in a definite age it has become "sensuous certainty" for Feuerbach.

Incidentally, when we conceive things thus, as they really are and happened, every profound philosophical problem is resolved, as will be seen even more clearly later, quite simply into an empirical fact. For instance, the important question of the relation of man to nature (Bruno [Bauer] goes so far as to speak of "the antitheses in nature and history" (p. 110), as though these were two separate "things" and man did not always have before him an historical nature and a natural history) out of which all the "unfathomably lofty works" on "substance" and "self-consciousness" were born, crumbles of itself when we understand that the celebrated "unity of man with nature" has always existed in industry and has existed in varying forms in every epoch according to the lesser or greater development of industry, just like the "struggle" of man with nature, right up to the development of his productive powers on a corresponding basis. Industry and commerce, production and the exchange of the necessities of life, themselves determine distribution, the structure of the different social classes and are, in turn, determined by it as to the mode in which they are carried on; and so it happens that in Manchester, for instance, Feuerbach sees only factories and machines, where a hundred years ago only spinning-wheels and weaving-looms were to be seen, or in the Campagna of Rome he finds only pasture lands and swamps, where in the time of Augustus he would have found nothing but the vineyards and villas of Roman capitalists. Feuerbach speaks in particular of the perception of natural science; he mentions secrets which are disclosed only to the eye of the physicist and chemist; but where would natural science be without industry and commerce? Even this "pure" natural science is provided with an aim, as with its material, only through trade and industry, through the sensuous activity of men. So much is this activity, this unceasing sensuous labour and creation, this production, the basis of the whole sensuous world as it now exists, that, were it interrupted only for a year, Feuerbach would not only find an enormous change in the natural world, but would very soon find that the whole world of men and his own perceptive faculty, nay his own existence, were missing. Of course, in all this the priority of external nature remains unassailed, and all this has no application to the original men produced by *generatio aequivoca*;[1] but this differentiation has meaning only insofar as man is considered to be distinct from nature. For that matter, nature, the nature that preceded human history, is not by any means the nature in which Feuerbach lives, it is nature which today no longer exists anywhere (except perhaps on a few Australian coral-islands of recent origin) and which, therefore, does not exist for Feuerbach.

Certainly Feuerbach has a great advantage over the "pure" materialists in that he realises how man too is an "object of the senses". But apart from the fact that he only conceives him as an "object of

[1] Spontaneous generation.—*Ed.*

the senses", not as "sensuous activity", because he still remains in the realm of theory and conceives of men not in their given social connection, not under their existing conditions of life, which have made them what they are, he never arrives at the really existing active men, but stops at the abstraction "man", and gets no further than recognising "the true, individual, corporeal man" emotionally, i.e. he knows no other "human relationships" "of man to man" than love and friendship, and even then idealised. He gives no criticism of the present conditions of life. Thus he never manages to conceive the sensuous world as the total living sensuous *activity* of the individuals composing it; and therefore when, for example, he sees instead of healthy men a crowd of scrofulous, overworked and consumptive starvelings, he is compelled to take refuge in the "higher perception" and in the ideal "compensation in the species", and thus to relapse into idealism at the very point where the communist materialist sees the necessity, and at the same time the condition, of a transformation both of industry and of the social structure.

As far as Feuerbach is a materialist he does not deal with history, and as far as he considers history he is not a materialist. With him materialism and history diverge completely, a fact which incidentally is already obvious from what has been said.

Ruling Class and Ruling Ideas

The ideas of the ruling class are in every epoch the ruling ideas, i.e. the class which is the ruling *material* force of society, is at the same time its ruling *intellectual* force. The class which has the means of material production at its disposal, has control at the same time over the means of mental production, so that thereby, generally speaking, the ideas of those who lack the means of mental production are subject to it. The ruling ideas are nothing more than the ideal expression of the dominant material relationships, the dominant material relationships grasped as ideas; hence of the relationships which make the one class the ruling one, therefore, the ideas of its dominance. The individuals composing the ruling class possess among other things consciousness, and therefore think. Insofar, therefore, as they rule as a class and determine the extent and compass of an epoch, it is self-evident that they do this in its whole range, hence among other things rule also as thinkers, as producers of ideas, and regulate the production and distribution of the ideas of their age: thus their ideas are the ruling ideas of the epoch. For instance, in an age and in a country where royal power, aristocracy, and bourgeoisie are contending for mastery and where, therefore, mastery is shared, the doctrine of the separation of powers proves to be the dominant idea and is expressed as an "eternal law".

The division of labour, which we already saw above (pp. [52–55]) as one of the chief forces of history up till now, manifests itself also in the ruling class as the division of mental and material labour, so that inside this class one part appears as the thinkers of the class (its active, conceptive ideologists, who make the perfecting of the illusion of the class about itself their chief source of livelihood), while the others' attitude to these ideas and illusions is more passive and receptive, because they are in reality the active members of this class and have less time to make up illusions and ideas about themselves. Within this class this cleavage can even develop into a certain opposition and hostility between the two parts, which, however, in the case of a practical collision, in which the class itself is endangered, automatically comes to nothing, in which case there also vanishes the semblance that the ruling ideas were not the ideas of the ruling class and had a power distinct from the power of this class. The existence of revolutionary ideas in a particular period presupposes the existence of a revolutionary class; about the premises for the latter sufficient has already been said above (pp. [54–57]).

If now in considering the course of history we detach the ideas of the ruling class from the ruling class itself and attribute to them an independent existence, if we confine ourselves to saying that these or those ideas were dominant at a given time, without bothering ourselves about the conditions of production and the producers of these ideas, if we thus ignore the individuals and world conditions which are the source of the ideas, we can say, for instance, that during the time that the aristocracy was dominant, the concepts honour, loyalty, etc. were dominant, during the dominance of the bourgeoisie the concepts freedom, equality, etc. The ruling class itself on the whole imagines this to be so. This conception of history, which is common to all historians, particularly since the eighteenth century, will necessarily come up against the phenomenon that increasingly abstract ideas hold sway, i.e. ideas which increasingly take on the form of universality. For each new class which puts itself in the place of one ruling before it, is compelled, merely in order to carry through its aim, to represent its interest as the common interest of all the members of society, that is, expressed in ideal form: it has to give its ideas the form of universality, and represent them as the only rational, universally valid ones. The class making a revolution appears from the very start, if only because it is opposed to a *class*, not as a class but as the representative of the whole of society; it appears as the whole mass of society confronting the one ruling class.[1] It can do this because, to start with, its interest really is more connected with the common interest of all other non-ruling classes, because under the pressure of hitherto existing conditions its interest has not yet been able to develop as the particular interest of a particular class. Its victory, therefore, benefits also many individuals of the other classes which are not winning a dominant position, but only insofar as it now puts these individuals in a position to raise themselves into the ruling class. When the French bourgeoisie overthrew the power of the aristocracy, it thereby made it possible for many proletarians to raise themselves above the proletariat, but only insofar as they become bourgeois. Every new class, therefore, achieves its hegemony only on a broader basis than that of the class ruling previously, whereas the opposition of the non-ruling class against the new ruling class later develops all the more sharply and profoundly. Both these things determine the fact that the struggle to be waged against this new ruling class, in its turn, aims at a more decided and radical negation of the previous conditions of society than could all previous classes which sought to rule.

This whole semblance, that the rule of a certain class is only the rule of certain ideas, comes to a natural end, of course, as soon as class rule in general ceases to be the form in which society is organised, that is to say, as soon as it is no longer necessary to represent a particular interest as general or the "general interest" as ruling.

Once the ruling ideas have been separated from the ruling individuals and, above all, from the relationships which result from a given stage of the mode of production, and in this way the conclusion has been reached that history is always under the sway of ideas, it is very easy to abstract from these various ideas "*the* idea", the notion, etc. as the dominant force in history, and thus to understand all these separate ideas and concepts as "forms of self-determination" on the part of

---

[1] [Marginal note by Marx:] Universality corresponds to (1) the class versus the estate, (2) the competition, world-wide intercourse, etc., (3) the great numerical strength of the ruling class, (4) the illusion of the *common* interests (in the beginning this illusion is true), (5) the delusion of the ideologists and the division of labour.

the concept developing in history. It follows then naturally, too, that all the relationships of men can be derived from the concept of man, man as conceived, the essence of man, *Man*. This has been done by the speculative philosophers. Hegel himself confesses at the end of the *Geschichtsphilosophie* that he "has considered the progress of the *concept* only" and has represented in history the "true *theodicy*". (p. 446.) Now one can go back again to the producers of the "concept", to the theorists, ideologists and philosophers, and one comes then to the conclusion that the philosophers, the thinkers as such, have at all times been dominant in history: a conclusion, as we see, already expressed by Hegel. The whole trick of proving the hegemony of the spirit in history (hierarchy Stirner calls it) is thus confined to the following three efforts.

No. 1. One must separate the ideas of those ruling for empirical reasons, under empirical conditions and as empirical individuals, from these actual rulers, and thus recognise the rule of ideas or illusions in history.

No. 2. One must bring an order into this rule of ideas, prove a mystical connection among the successive ruling ideas, which is managed by understanding them as "acts of self-determination on the part of the concept" (this is possible because by virtue of their empirical basis these ideas are really connected with one another and because, conceived as *mere* ideas, they become self-distinctions, distinctions made by thought).

No. 3. To remove the mystical appearance of this "self-determining concept" it is changed into a person—"Self-Consciousness"—or, to appear thoroughly materialistic, into a series of persons, who represent the "concept" in history, into the "thinkers", the "philosophers", the ideologists, who again are understood as the manufacturers of history, as the "council of guardians", as the rulers. Thus the whole body of materialistic elements has been removed from history and now full rein can be given to the speculative steed.

Whilst in ordinary life every shopkeeper is very well able to distinguish between what somebody professes to be and what he really is, our historians have not yet won even this trivial insight. They take every epoch at its word and believe that everything it says and imagines about itself is true.

This historical method which reigned in Germany, and especially the reason why, must be understood from its connection with the illusion of ideologists in general, e.g. the illusions of the jurist, politicians (of the practical statesmen among them, too), from the dogmatic dreamings and distortions of these fellows; this is explained perfectly easily from their practical position in life, their job, and the division of labour.

C. THE REAL BASIS OF IDEOLOGY

Division of Labour: Town and Country

[. . . .][1] From the first there follows the premise of a highly developed division of labour and an extensive commerce; from the second, the locality. In the first case the individuals must be brought together; in the second they find themselves alongside the given instrument of production as instruments of production themselves. Here, therefore, arises the difference between natural instruments of production and those created by civilisation. The field (water, etc.) can be regarded as a natural instrument of production. In the first case, that of the natural instrument of production, individuals are subservient to nature; in the second, to a product of labour. In the first case, therefore, property (landed property) appears as direct natural domination, in the second, as domination of labour, particularly of accumulated labour, capital. The first case presupposes that the individuals are united by some bond: family, tribe, the land itself, etc.; the second, that they are independent of one another and are only held together by exchange. In the first case, what is involved is chiefly an exchange between men and nature in which the labour of the former is exchanged for the products of the latter; in the second, it is predominantly an exchange of men among themselves. In the first case, average, human common sense is adequate—physical activity is as yet not separated from mental activity; in the second, the division between physical and mental labour must already be practically completed. In the first case, the domination of the proprietor over the propertyless may be based on a personal relationship, on a kind of community; in the second, it must have taken on a material shape in a third party—money. In the first case, small industry exists, but determined by the utilisation of the natural instrument of production and therefore without the distribution of labour among various individuals; in the second, industry exists only in and through the division of labour.

The greatest division of material and mental labour is the separation

---

[1] Four pages of the manuscript are missing here.—*Ed.*

of town and country. The antagonism between town and country begins with the transition from barbarism to civilisation, from tribe to State, from locality to nation, and runs through the whole history of civilisation to the present day (the Anti-Corn Law League).

The existence of the town implies, at the same time, the necessity of administration, police, taxes, etc.; in short, of the municipality, and thus of politics in general. Here first became manifest the division of the population into two great classes, which is directly based on the division of labour and on the instruments of production. The town already is in actual fact the concentration of the population, of the instruments of production, of capital, of pleasures, of needs, while the country demonstrates just the opposite fact, isolation and separation. The antagonism between town and country can only exist within the framework of private property. It is the most crass expression of the subjection of the individual under the division of labour, under a definite activity forced upon him—a subjection which makes one man into a restricted town-animal, the other into a restricted country-animal, and daily creates anew the conflict between their interests. Labour is here again the chief thing, power *over* individuals, and as long as the latter exists, private property must exist. The abolition of the antagonism between town and country is one of the first conditions of communal life, a condition which again depends on a mass of material premises and which cannot be fulfilled by the mere will, as anyone can see at the first glance. (These conditions have still to be enumerated.) The separation of town and country can also be understood as the separation of capital and landed property, as the beginning of the existence and development of capital independent of landed property—the beginning of property having its basis only in labour and exchange.

In the towns which, in the Middle Ages, did not derive ready-made from an earlier period but were formed anew by the serfs who had become free, each man's own particular labour was his only property apart from the small capital he brought with him, consisting almost solely of the most necessary tools of his craft. The competition of serfs constantly escaping into the town, the constant war of the country against the towns and thus the necessity of an organised municipal military force, the bond of common ownership in a particular kind of labour, the necessity of common buildings for the sale of their wares at a time when craftsmen were also traders, and the consequent exclusion of the unauthorised from these buildings, the conflict among the interests of the various crafts, the necessity of protecting their laboriously acquired skill, and the feudal organisation of the whole of the country: these were the causes of the union of the workers of each craft in guilds. We have not at this point to go further into the manifold modifications of the guild-system, which arise through later historical developments. The flight of the serfs into the towns went on without interruption right through the Middle Ages. These serfs, persecuted by their lords in the country, came separately into the towns, where they found an organised community, against which they were powerless and in which they had to subject themselves to the station assigned to them by the demand for their labour and the interest of their organised urban competitors. These workers, entering separately, were never able to attain to any power, since, if their labour was of the guild type which had to be learned, the guild-masters bent them to their will and organised them according to their interest; or if their labour was not such as had to be learned, and therefore not of the guild type, they became day-labourers and never managed to organise, remaining an unorganised rabble. The need for day-labourers in the towns created the rabble.

These towns were true "associations", called forth by the direct need, the care of providing for the protection of property, and of multiplying the means of production and defence of the separate members. The rabble of these towns was devoid of any power, composed as it was of individuals strange to one another who had entered separately, and who stood unorganised over against an organised power, armed for war, and jealously watching over them. The journeymen and apprentices were organised in each craft as it best suited the interest of the masters. The patriarchal relationship existing between them and their masters gave the latter a double power—on the one hand because of their influence on the whole life of the journeymen, and on the other because, for the journeymen who worked with the same master, it was a real bond which held them together against the journeymen of other masters and separated them from these. And finally, the journeymen were bound to the existing order by their simple interest in becoming masters themselves. While, therefore, the rabble at least carried out revolts against the whole municipal order, revolts which remained completely ineffective because of their powerlessness, the journeymen never got further than small acts of insubordination within separate guilds, such as belong to the very nature of the guild-system. The great risings of the Middle

Ages all radiated from the country, but equally remained totally ineffective because of the isolation and consequent crudity of the peasants.

In the towns, the division of labour between the individual guilds was as yet [quite naturally derived] and, in the guilds themselves, not at all developed between the individual workers. Every workman had to be versed in a whole round of tasks, had to be able to make everything that was to be made with his tools. The limited commerce and the scanty communication between the individual towns, the lack of population and the narrow needs did not allow of a higher division of labour, and therefore every man who wished to become a master had to be proficient in the whole of his craft. Thus there is found with medieval craftsmen an interest in their special work and in proficiency in it, which was capable of rising to a narrow artistic sense. For this very reason, however, every medieval craftsman was completely absorbed in his work, to which he had a contented, slavish relationship, and to which he was subjected to a far greater extent than the modern worker, whose work is a matter of indifference to him.

Capital in these towns was a naturally derived capital, consisting of a house, the tools of the craft, and the natural, hereditary customers; and not being realisable, on account of the backwardness of commerce and the lack of circulation, it descended from father to son. Unlike modern capital, which can be assessed in money and which may be indifferently invested in this thing or that, this capital was directly connected with the particular work of the owner, inseparable from it and to this extent *estate* capital.

The next extension of the division of labour was the separation of production and commerce, the formation of a special class of merchants; a separation which, in the towns bequeathed by a former period, had been handed down (among other things with the Jews) and which very soon appeared in the newly formed ones. With this there was given the possibility of commercial communications transcending the immediate neighbourhood, a possibility, the realisation of which depended on the existing means of communication, the state of public safety in the countryside, which was determined by political conditions (during the whole of the Middle Ages, as is well known, the merchants travelled in armed caravans), and on the cruder or more advanced needs (determined by the stage of culture attained) of the region accessible to intercourse.

With commerce the prerogative of a particular class, with the extension of trade through the merchants beyond the immediate surroundings of the town, there immediately appears a reciprocal action between production and commerce. The towns enter into relations *with one another*, new tools are brought from one town into the other, and the separation between production and commerce soon calls forth a new division of production between the individual towns, each of which is soon exploiting a predominant branch of industry. The local restrictions of earlier times begin gradually to be broken down.

It depends purely on the extension of commerce whether the productive forces achieved in a locality, especially inventions, are lost for later development or not. As long as there exists no commerce transcending the immediate neighbourhood, every invention must be made separately in each locality, and mere chances such as irruptions of barbaric peoples, even ordinary wars, are sufficient to cause a country with advanced productive forces and needs to have to start right over again from the beginning. In primitive history every invention had to be made daily anew and in each locality independently. How little highly developed productive forces are safe from complete destruction, given even a relatively very extensive commerce, is proved by the Phoenicians, whose inventions were for the most part lost for a long time to come through the ousting of this nation from commerce, its conquest by Alexander and its consequent decline. Likewise, for instance, glass-painting in the Middle Ages. Only when commerce has become world commerce and has as its basis large-scale industry, when all nations are drawn into the competitive struggle, is the permanence of the acquired productive forces assured.

The Rise of Manufacturing

The immediate consequence of the division of labour between the various towns was the rise of manufactures, branches of production which had outgrown the guild-system. Manufactures first flourished, in Italy and later in Flanders, under the historical premise of commerce with foreign nations. In other countries, England and France for example, manufactures were at first confined to the home market. Besides the premises already mentioned manufactures depend on an already advanced concentration of population, particularly in the countryside, and of capital, which began to accumulate in the hands of individuals, partly in the guilds in spite of the guild regulations, partly among the merchants.

That labour which from the first presupposed a machine, even of the crudest sort, soon showed itself the most capable of development. Weaving, earlier carried on in the country by the peasants as a secondary occupation to procure their clothing, was the first labour to receive an impetus and a further development through the extension of commerce. Weaving was the first and remained the principal manufacture. The rising demand for clothing materials, consequent on the growth of population, the growing accumulation and mobilisation of natural capital through accelerated circulation, the demand for luxuries called forth by the latter and favoured generally by the gradual extension of commerce, gave weaving a quantitative and qualitative stimulus, which wrenched it out of the form of production hitherto existing. Alongside the peasants weaving for their own use, who continued, and still continue, with this sort of work, there emerged a new class of weavers in the towns, whose fabrics were destined for the whole home market and usually for foreign markets too.

Weaving, an occupation demanding in most cases little skill and soon splitting up into countless branches, by its whole nature resisted the trammels of the guild. Weaving was, therefore, carried on mostly in villages and market-centres without guild organisation, which gradually became towns, and indeed the most flourishing towns in each land.

With guild-free manufacture, property relations also quickly changed. The first advance beyond naturally derived estate capital was provided by the rise of merchants whose capital was from the beginning movable, capital in the modern sense as far as one can speak of it, given the circumstances of those times. The second advance came with manufacture, which again made mobile a mass of natural capital, and altogether increased the mass of movable capital as against that of natural capital.

At the same time, manufacture became a refuge of the peasants from the guilds which excluded them or paid them badly, just as earlier the guild-towns had [served] as a refuge for the peasants from [the oppressive landed nobility].

Simultaneously with the beginning of manufactures there was a period of vagabondage caused by the abolition of the feudal bodies of retainers, the disbanding of the swollen armies which had flocked to serve the kings against their vassals, the improvement of agriculture, and the transformation of great strips of tillage into pasture land.

From this alone it is clear how this vagabondage is strictly connected with the disintegration of the feudal system. As early as the thirteenth century we find isolated epochs of this kind, but only at the end of the fifteenth and beginning of the sixteenth does this vagabondage make a general and permanent appearance. These vagabonds, who were so numerous that, for instance, Henry VIII of England had 72,000 of them hanged, were only prevailed upon to work with the greatest difficulty and through the most extreme necessity, and then only after long resistance. The rapid rise of manufactures, particularly in England, absorbed them gradually.

With the advent of manufactures, the various nations entered into a competitive relationship, the struggle for trade, which was fought out in wars, protective duties and prohibitions, whereas earlier the nations, insofar as they were connected at all, had carried on an inoffensive exchange with each other. Trade had from now on a political significance.

With the advent of manufacture the relationship between worker and employer changed. In the guilds the patriarchal relationship between journeyman and master continued to exist; in manufacture its place was taken by the monetary relation between worker and capitalist—a relationship which in the countryside and in small towns retained a patriarchal tinge, but in the larger, the real manufacturing towns, quite early lost almost all patriarchal complexion.

Manufacture and the movement of production in general received an enormous impetus through the extension of commerce which came with the discovery of America and the sea-route to the East Indies. The new products imported thence, particularly the masses of gold and silver which came into circulation and totally changed the position of the classes towards one another, dealing a hard blow to feudal landed property and to the workers; the expeditions of adventurers, colonisation; and above all the extension of markets into a world market, which had now become possible and was daily becoming more and more a fact, called forth a new phase of historical development, into which in general we cannot here enter further. Through the colonisation of the newly discovered countries the commercial struggle of the nations amongst one another was given new fuel and accordingly greater extension and animosity.

The expansion of trade and manufacture accelerated the accumulation of movable capital, while in the guilds, which were not stimulated to extend their production, natural capital remained stationary or even declined. Trade and manufacture created the big bourgeoisie; in the guilds was concentrated the petty bourgeoisie, which no longer was dominant in the towns as formerly, but had to bow to the might of the great merchants and manufacturers. Hence the decline of the guilds, as soon as they came into contact with manufacture.

The intercourse of nations took on, in the epoch of which we have been speaking, two different forms. At first the small quantity of gold and silver in circulation involved the ban on the export of these metals; and industry, for the most part imported from abroad and made necessary by the need for employing the growing urban population, could not do without those privileges which could be granted not only, of course, against home competition, but chiefly against foreign. The local guild privilege was in these original prohibitions extended over the whole nation. Customs duties originated from the tributes which the feudal lords exacted as protective levies against robbery from merchants passing through their territories, tributes later imposed likewise by the towns, and which, with the rise of the modern states, were the Treasury's most obvious means of raising money.

The appearance of American gold and silver on the European markets, the gradual development of industry, the rapid expansion of trade and the consequent rise of the non-guild bourgeoisie and of money, gave these measures another significance. The State, which was daily less and less able to do without money, now retained the ban on the export of gold and silver out of fiscal considerations; the bourgeois, for whom these masses of money which were hurled onto the market became the chief object of speculative buying, were thoroughly content with this; privileges established earlier became a source of income for the government and were sold for money; in the customs legislation there appeared the export duty, which, since it only [placed] a hindrance in the way of industry, had a purely fiscal aim.

The second period began in the middle of the seventeenth century and lasted almost to the end of the eighteenth. Commerce and navigation had expanded more rapidly than manufacture, which played a secondary role; the colonies were becoming considerable consumers; and after long struggles the separate nations shared out the opening world market among themselves. This period begins with the Navigation Laws[1] and colonial monopolies. The competition of the

---

[1] *Navigation Laws*—a series of Acts passed in England from 1381 onwards to protect English shipping against foreign competition. The best known was that of 1651, directed

nations among themselves was excluded as far as possible by tariffs, prohibitions and treaties; and in the last resort the competitive struggle was carried on and decided by wars (especially naval wars). The mightiest maritime nation, the English, retained preponderance in trade and manufacture. Here, already, we find concentration in one country.

Manufacture was all the time sheltered by protective duties in the home market, by monopolies in the colonial market, and abroad as much as possible by differential duties. The working-up of home-produced material was encouraged (wool and linen in England, silk in France), the export of home-produced raw material forbidden (wool in England), and the [working-up] of imported material neglected or suppressed (cotton in England). The nation dominant in sea trade and colonial power naturally secured for itself also the greatest quantitative and qualitative expansion of manufacture. Manufacture could not be carried on without protection, since, if the slightest change takes place in other countries, it can lose its market and be ruined; under reasonably favourable conditions it may easily be introduced into a country, but for this very reason can easily be destroyed. At the same time through the mode in which it is carried on, particularly in the eighteenth century, in the countryside, it is to such an extent interwoven with the vital relationships of a great mass of individuals, that no country dare jeopardise its existence by permitting free competition. Insofar as it manages to export, it therefore depends entirely on the extension or restriction of commerce, and exercises a relatively very small reaction [on the latter]. Hence its secondary [importance] and the influence of [the merchants] in the eighteenth century. It was the merchants and especially the shippers who more than anybody else pressed for State protection and monopolies; the manufacturers also demanded and indeed received protection, but all the time were inferior in political importance to the merchants. The commercial towns, particularly the maritime towns, became to some extent civilised and acquired the outlook of the big bourgeoisie, but in the factory towns an extreme petty-bourgeois outlook persisted. Cf. Aikin,[1] etc. The eighteenth century was the

mainly against the Dutch, who controlled most of the carrying trade. It prohibited the importation of any goods not carried in English ships or the ships of the country where the goods were produced, and laid down that British coasting trade and commerce with the colonies was to be carried on only by English boats. The Navigation Laws were modified in the early nineteenth century and repealed in 1849 except for a reservation regarding coasting trade, which was revoked in 1854.—Ed.

[1] The movement of capital, although considerably accelerated, still remained, however,

century of trade. Pinto says this expressly: *"Le commerce fait la marotte du siècle"*;[1] and: *"Depuis quelque temps il n'est plus question que de commerce, de navigation et de marine."*[2]

This period is also characterised by the cessation of the bans on the export of gold and silver and the beginning of the trade in money; by banks, national debts, paper money; by speculation in stocks and shares and stockjobbing in all articles; by the development of finance in general. Again capital lost a great part of the natural character which had still clung to it.

The concentration of trade and manufacture in one country, England, developing irresistibly in the seventeenth century, gradually created for this country a relative world market, and thus a demand for the manufactured products of this country, which could no longer be met by the industrial productive forces hitherto existing. This demand, outgrowing the productive forces, was the motive power which, by producing big industry—the application of elemental forces to industrial ends, machinery and the most complex division of labour—called into existence the third period of private ownership since the Middle Ages. There already existed in England the other pre-conditions of this new phase: freedom of competition inside the nation, the development of theoretical mechanics, etc. (Indeed, the science of mechanics perfected by Newton was altogether the most popular science in France and England in the eighteenth century.) (Free competition inside the nation itself had everywhere to be conquered by a revolution—1640 and 1688 in England, 1789 in France.) Competition soon compelled every country that wished to retain its historical role to protect its manufactures by renewed customs regulations (the old duties were no longer any good against big industry) and soon after to introduce big industry under protective duties. Big industry universalised competition in spite of these protective measures (it is practical free trade; the protective duty is only a

relatively slow. The splitting-up of the world market into separate parts, each of which was exploited by a particular nation, the exclusion of competition among themselves on the part of the nations, the clumsiness of production itself and the fact that finance was only evolving from its early stages, greatly impeded circulation. The consequence of this was a haggling, mean and niggardly spirit which still clung to all merchants and to the whole mode of carrying on trade. Compared with the manufacturers, and above all with the craftsmen, they were certainly big bourgeois; compared with the merchants and industrialists of the next period they remain petty bourgeois. Cf. Adam Smith.

[1] "Commerce is the rage of the century."—*Ed.*

[2] "For some time now people have been talking only about commerce, navigation and the navy."—*Ed.*

palliative, a measure of defence *within* free trade), established means of communication and the modern world market, subordinated trade to itself, transformed all capital into industrial capital, and thus produced the rapid circulation (development of the financial system) and the centralisation of capital. By universal competition it forced all individuals to strain their energy to the utmost. It destroyed as far as possible ideology, religion, morality, etc. and where it could not do this, made them into a palpable lie. It produced world history for the first time, insofar as it made all civilised nations and every individual member of them dependent for the satisfaction of their wants on the whole world, thus destroying the former natural exclusiveness of separate nations. It made natural science subservient to capital and took from the division of labour the last semblance of its natural character. It destroyed natural growth in general, as far as this is possible while labour exists, and resolved all natural relationships into money relationships. In the place of naturally grown towns it created the modern, large industrial cities which have sprung up overnight. Wherever it penetrated, it destroyed the crafts and all earlier stages of industry. It completed the victory of the commercial town over the countryside. [Its first premise] was the automatic system. [Its development] produced a mass of productive forces, for which private [property] became just as much a fetter as the guild had been for manufacture and the small, rural workshop for the developing craft. These productive forces received under the system of private property a one-sided development only, and became for the majority destructive forces; moreover, a great multitude of such forces could find no application at all within this system. Generally speaking, big industry created everywhere the same relations between the classes of society, and thus destroyed the peculiar individuality of the various nationalities. And finally, while the bourgeoisie of each nation still retained separate national interests, big industry created a class, which in all nations has the same interest and with which nationality is already dead; a class which is really rid of all the old world and at the same time stands pitted against it. Big industry makes for the worker not only the relation to the capitalist, but labour itself, unbearable.

It is evident that big industry does not reach the same level of development in all districts of a country. This does not, however, retard the class movement of the proletariat, because the proletarians created by big industry assume leadership of this movement and carry the whole mass along with them, and because the workers excluded from big industry are placed by it in a still worse situation than the workers in big industry itself. The countries in which big industry is developed act in a similar manner upon the more or less non-industrial countries, insofar as the latter are swept by universal commerce into the universal competitive struggle.[1]

These different forms are just so many forms of the organisation of labour, and hence of property. In each period a unification of the existing productive forces takes place, insofar as this has been rendered necessary by needs.

The Relation of State and Law to Property

The first form of property, in the ancient world as in the Middle Ages, is tribal property, determined with the Romans chiefly by war, with the Germans by the rearing of cattle. In the case of the ancient peoples, since several tribes live together in one town, the tribal property appears as State property, and the right of the individual to it as mere "possession" which, however, like tribal property as a whole, is confined to landed property only. Real private property began with the ancients, as with modern nations, with movable property.—(Slavery and community) (*dominium ex jure Quiritum*[2]). In the case of the nations which grew out of the Middle Ages, tribal property evolved through various stages—feudal landed property, corporative movable property, capital invested in manufacture—to modern capital, determined by big industry and universal competition, i.e. pure private property, which has cast off all semblance of a communal institution and has shut out the State from any influence on the development of property. To this modern private property corresponds the modern State, which, purchased gradually by the owners of property by means of taxation, has fallen entirely into their hands through the national debt, and its existence has become wholly

[1] Competition separates individuals from one another, not only the bourgeois but still more the workers, in spite of the fact that it brings them together. Hence it is a long time before these individuals can unite, apart from the fact that for the purposes of this union— if it is not to be merely local—the necessary means, the great industrial cities and cheap and quick communications, have first to be produced by big industry. Hence every organised power standing over against these isolated individuals, who live in relationships, daily reproducing this isolation, can only be overcome after long struggles. To demand the opposite would be tantamount to demanding that competition should not exist in this definite epoch of history, or that the individuals should banish from their minds relationships over which in their isolation they have no control.

[2] Ownership in accordance with the law applying to full Roman citizens.—*Ed.*

dependent on the commercial credit which the owners of property, the bourgeois, extend to it, as reflected in the rise and fall of State funds on the stock exchange. By the mere fact that it is a *class* and no longer an *estate*, the bourgoisie is forced to organize itself no longer locally, but nationally, and to give a general form to its mean average interest. Through the emancipation of private property from the community, the State has become a separate entity, beside and outside civil society; but it is nothing more than the form of organisation which the bourgeois necessarily adopt both for internal and external purposes, for the mutual guarantee of their property and interests. The independence of the State is only found nowadays in those countries where the estates have not yet completely developed into classes, where the estates, done away with in more advanced countries, still have a part to play, and where there exists a mixture; countries, that is to say, in which no one section of the population can achieve dominance over the others. This is the case particularly in Germany. The most perfect example of the modern State is North America. The modern French, English and American writers all express the opinion that the State exists only for the sake of private property, so that this fact has penetrated into the consciousness of the normal man.

Since the State is the form in which the individuals of a ruling class assert their common interests, and in which the whole civil society of an epoch is epitomised, it follows that the State mediates in the formation of all common institutions and that the institutions receive a political form. Hence the illusion that law is based on the will, and indeed on the will divorced from its real basis—on *free* will. Similarly, justice is in its turn reduced to the actual laws.

Civil law develops simultaneously with private property out of the disintegration of the natural community. With the Romans the development of private property and civil law had no further industrial and commercial consequences, because their whole mode of production did not alter. (Usury!)

With modern peoples, where the feudal community was disintegrated by industry and trade, there began with the rise of private property and civil law a new phase, which was capable of further development. The very first town which carried on an extensive maritime trade in the Middle Ages, Amalfi, also developed maritime law. As soon as industry and trade developed private property further, first in Italy and later in other countries, the highly developed Roman civil law was immediately adopted again and raised to authority. When later the bourgeoisie had acquired so much power that the princes took up its interests in order to overthrow the feudal nobility by means of the bourgeoisie, there began in all countries—in France in the sixteenth century—the real development of law, which in all countries except England proceeded on the basis of the Roman Codex. In England, too, Roman legal principles had to be introduced to further the development of civil law (especially in the case of movable property). (It must not be forgotten that law has just as little an independent history as religion.)

In civil law the existing property relationships are declared to be the result of the general will. The *jus utendi et abutendi*[1] itself asserts on the one hand the fact that private property has become entirely independent of the community, and on the other the illusion that private property itself is based solely on the private will, the arbitrary disposal of the thing. In practice, the *abuti*[1] has very definite economic limitations for the owner of private property, if he does not wish to see his property and hence his *jus abutendi* pass into other hands, since actually the thing, considered merely with reference to his will, is not a thing at all, but only becomes a thing, true property in intercourse, and independently of the law (a *relationship*, which the philosophers call an idea). This juridical illusion, which reduces law to the mere will, necessarily leads, in the further development of property relationships, to the position that a man may have a legal title to a thing without really having the thing. If, for instance, the income from a piece of land is lost owing to competition, then the proprietor has certainly his legal title to it along with the *jus utendi et abutendi*. But he can do nothing with it: he owns nothing as a landed proprietor if in addition he has not enough capital to cultivate his ground. This illusion of the jurists also explains the fact that for them, as for every code, it is altogether fortuitous that individuals enter into relationships among themselves (e.g. contracts); it explains why they consider that these relationships [can] be entered into or not at will, and that their content rests purely on the individual [free] will of the contracting parties.

Whenever, through the development of industry and commerce, new forms of intercourse have been evolved (e.g. assurance companies, etc.), the law has always been compelled to admit them among the modes of acquiring property.

---

[1] The right of using and consuming (also: abusing), i.e. of disposing of a thing at will.—*Ed.*

D. PROLETARIANS AND COMMUNISM

Individuals, Class, and Community

In the Middle Ages the citizens in each town were compelled to unite against the landed nobility to save their skins. The extension of trade, the establishment of communications, led the separate towns to get to know other towns, which had asserted the same interests in the struggle with the same antagonist. Out of the many local corporations of burghers there arose only gradually the burgher *class*. The conditions of life of the individual burghers became, on account of their contradiction to the existing relationships and of the mode of labour determined by these, conditions which were common to them all and independent of each individual. The burghers had created the conditions insofar as they had torn themselves free from feudal ties, and were created by them insofar as they were determined by their antagonism to the feudal system which they found in existence. When the individual towns began to enter into associations, these common conditions developed into class conditions. The same conditions, the same contradiction, the same interests necessarily called forth on the whole similar customs everywhere. The bourgeoisie itself, with its conditions, develops only gradually, splits according to the division of labour into various fractions and finally absorbs all propertied classes it finds in existence[1] (while it develops the majority of the earlier propertyless and a part of the hitherto propertied classes into a new class, the proletariat) in the measure to which all property found in existence is transformed into industrial or commercial capital. The separate individuals form a class only insofar as they have to carry on a common battle against another class; otherwise they are on hostile terms with each other as competitors. On the other hand, the class in its turn achieves an independent existence over against the individuals, so that the latter find their conditions of existence predestined, and hence have their position in life and their personal development assigned to them by their class, become subsumed under it. This is the same phenomenon as the subjection of the separate individuals to the division of labour and can only be removed by the abolition of private property and of labour itself. We have already indicated several times how this subsuming of individuals under the class brings with it their subjection to all kinds of ideas, etc.

[1] [Marginal note by Marx:] To begin with it absorbs the branches of labour directly belonging to the State and then all ± [more or less] ideological estates.

If from a *philosophical* point of view one considers this evolution of individuals in the common conditions of existence of estates and classes, which followed on one another, and in the accompanying general conceptions forced upon them, it is certainly very easy to imagine that in these individuals the species, or "Man", has evolved, or that they evolved "Man"—and in this way one can give history some hard clouts on the ear.[1] One can conceive these various estates and classes to be specific terms of the general expression, subordinate varieties of the species, or evolutionary phases of "Man".

This subsuming of individuals under definite classes cannot be abolished until a class has taken shape, which has no longer any particular class interest to assert against the ruling class.

The transformation, through the division of labour, of personal powers (relationships) into material powers, cannot be dispelled by dismissing the general idea of it from one's mind, but can only be abolished by the individuals again subjecting these material powers to themselves and abolishing the division of labour. This is not possible without the community. Only in community [with others has each] individual the means of cultivating his gifts in all directions; only in the community, therefore, is personal freedom possible. In the previous substitutes for the community, in the State, etc. personal freedom has existed only for the individuals who developed within the relationships of the ruling class, and only insofar as they were individuals of this class. The illusory community, in which individuals have up till now combined, always took on an independent existence in relation to them, and was at the same time, since it was the combination of one class over against another, not only a completely illusory community, but a new fetter as well. In a real community the individuals obtain their freedom in and through their association.

Individuals have always built on themselves, but naturally on themselves within their given historical conditions and relationships, not on the "pure" individual in the sense of the ideologists. But in the course of historical evolution, and precisely through the inevitable fact that within the division of labour social relationships take on an independent existence, there appears a division within the life of each individual, insofar as it is personal and insofar as it is determined

[1] The statement which frequently occurs with Saint Max that each is all that he is through the State is fundamentally the same as the statement that bourgeois is only a specimen of the bourgeois species; a statement which presupposes that the *class* of bourgeois existed before the individuals constituting it. [Marginal note by Marx to this sentence:] With the philosophers *pre-existence* of the class.

by some branch of labour and the conditions pertaining to it. (We do not mean it to be understood from this that, for example, the rentier, the capitalist, etc. cease to be persons; but their personality is conditioned and determined by quite definite class relationships, and the division appears only in their opposition to another class and, for themselves, only when they go bankrupt.) In the estate (and even more in the tribe) this is as yet concealed: for instance, a nobleman always remains a nobleman, a commoner always a commoner, apart from his other relationships, a quality inseparable from his individuality. The division between the personal and the class individual, the accidental nature of the conditions of life for the individual, appears only with the emergence of the class, which is itself a product of the bourgeoisie. This accidental character is only engendered and developed by competition and the struggle of individuals among themselves. Thus, in imagination, individuals seem freer under the dominance of the bourgeoisie than before, because their conditions of life seem accidental; in reality, of course, they are less free, because they are more subjected to the violence of things. The difference from the estate comes out particularly in the antagonism between the bourgeoisie and the proletariat. When the estate of the urban burghers, the corporations, etc. emerged in opposition to the landed nobility, their condition of existence—movable property and craft labour, which had already existed latently before their separation from the feudal ties—appeared as something positive, which was asserted against feudal landed property, and, therefore, in its own way at first took on a feudal form. Certainly the refugee serfs treated their previous servitude as something accidental to their personality. But here they only were doing what every class that is freeing itself from a fetter does; and they did not free themselves as a class but separately. Moreover, they did not rise above the system of estates, but only formed a new estate, retaining their previous mode of labour even in their new situation, and developing it further by freeing it from its earlier fetters, which no longer corresponded to the development already attained.[1]

[1] N.B.—It must not be forgotten that the serf's very need of existing and the impossibility of a large-scale economy, which involved the distribution of the allotments among the serfs, very soon reduced the services of the serfs to their lord to an average of payments in kind and statute-labour. This made it possible for the serf to accumulate movable property and hence facilitated his escape out of the possession of his lord and gave him the prospect of making his way as an urban citizen; it also created gradations among the serfs, so that the runaway serfs were already half burghers. It is likewise obvious that the serfs who were masters of a craft had the best chance of acquiring movable property.

For the proletarians, on the other hand, the condition of their existence, labour, and with it all the conditions of existence governing modern society, have become something accidental, something over which they, as separate individuals, have no control, and over which no *social* organisation can give them control. The contradiction between the individuality of each separate proletarian and labour, the condition of life forced upon him, becomes evident to him himself, for he is sacrificed from youth upwards and, within his own class, has no chance of arriving at the conditions which would place him in the other class.

Thus, while the refugee serfs only wished to be free to develop and assert those conditions of existence which were already there, and hence, in the end, only arrived at free labour, the proletarians, if they are to assert themselves as individuals, will have to abolish the very condition of their existence hitherto (which has, moreover, been that of all society up to the present), namely, labour. Thus they find themselves directly opposed to the form in which, hitherto, the individuals, of which society consists, have given themselves collective expression, that is, the State. In order, therefore, to assert themselves as individuals, they must overthrow the State.

It follows from all we have been saying up till now that the communal relationship into which the individuals of a class entered, and which was determined by their common interests over against a third party, was always a community to which these individuals belonged only as average individuals, only insofar as they lived within the conditions of existence of their class—a relationship in which they participated not as individuals but as members of a class. With the community of revolutionary proletarians, on the other hand, who take their conditions of existence and those of all members of society under their control, it is just the reverse; it is as individuals that the individuals participate in it. It is just this combination of individuals (assuming the advanced stage of modern productive forces, of course) which puts the conditions of the free development and movement of individuals under their control—conditions which were previously abandoned to chance and had won an independent existence over against the separate individuals just because of their separation as individuals, and because of the necessity of their combination which had been determined by the division of labour, and through their separation had become a bond alien to them. Combination up till now (by no means an arbitrary one, such as is expounded for example in the *Contrat social*, but a necessary one) was an agreement upon these conditions, within which the individuals were free to enjoy the freaks of fortune (compare, e.g., the formation of the North American State and the South American republics). This right to the undisturbed enjoyment, within certain conditions, of fortuity and chance has up till now been called personal freedom. These conditions of existence are, of course, only the productive forces and forms of intercourse at any particular time.

Forms of Intercourse

Communism differs from all previous movements in that it overturns the basis of all earlier relations of production and intercourse, and for the first time consciously treats all natural premises as the creatures of hitherto existing men, strips them of their natural character and subjugates them to the power of the united individuals. Its organisation is, therefore, essentially economic, the material production of the conditions of this unity; it turns existing conditions into conditions of unity. The reality, which communism is creating, is precisely the true basis for rendering it impossible that anything should exist independently of individuals, insofar as reality is only a product of the preceding intercourse of individuals themselves. Thus the communists in practice treat the conditions created up to now by production and intercourse as inorganic conditions, without, however, imagining that it was the plan or the destiny of previous generations to give them material, and without believing that these conditions were inorganic for the individuals creating them. The difference between the individual as a person and what is accidental to him, is not a conceptual difference but an historical fact. This distinction has a different significance at different times—e.g. the estate as something accidental to the individual in the eighteenth century, the family more or less too. It is not a distinction that we have to make for each age, but one which each age makes itself from among the different elements which it finds in existence, and indeed not according to any theory, but compelled by material collisions in life. What appears accidental to the later age as opposed to the earlier—and this applies also to the elements handed down by an earlier age—is a form of intercourse which corresponded to a definite stage of development of the productive forces. The relation of the productive forces to the form of intercourse is the relation of the form of intercourse to the occupation or activity of the individuals. (The fundamental form of this activity is, of course, material, on which depend all other forms—mental, political, religious, etc. The various shaping of material life is, of course, in every case dependent on the needs which are already developed, and the production, as well as the satisfaction, of these needs is an historical process, which is not found in the case of a sheep or a dog (Stirner's refractory principal argument *adversus hominem*), although sheep and dogs in their present form certainly, but *malgré eux*, are products of an historical process.) The conditions under which individuals have intercourse with each other, so long as the above-mentioned contradiction is absent, are conditions appertaining to their individuality, in no way external to them; conditions under which these definite individuals, living under definite relationships, can alone produce their material life and what is connected with it, are thus the conditions of their self-activity and are produced by this self-activity. The definite condition under which they produce, thus corresponds, as long as the contradiction has not yet appeared, to the reality of their conditioned nature, their one-sided existence, the one-sidedness of which only becomes evident when the contradiction enters on the scene and thus exists for the later individuals. Then this condition appears as an accidental fetter, and the consciousness that it is a fetter is imputed to the earlier age as well.

These various conditions, which appear first as conditions of self-activity, later as fetters upon it, form in the whole evolution of history a coherent series of forms of intercourse, the coherence of which consists in this: in the place of an earlier form of intercourse, which has become a fetter, a new one is put, corresponding to the more developed productive forces and, hence, to the advanced mode of the self-activity of individuals—a form which in its turn becomes a fetter and is then replaced by another. Since these conditions correspond at every stage to the simultaneous development of the productive forces, their history is at the same time the history of the evolving productive forces taken over by each new generation, and is, therefore, the history of the development of the forces of the individuals themselves.

Since this evolution takes place naturally, i.e. is not subordinated to a general plan of freely combined individuals, it proceeds from various localities, tribes, nations, branches of labour, etc. each of which to start with develops independently of the others and only gradually enters into relation with the others. Furthermore, it takes place only very slowly; the various stages and interests are never completely overcome, but only subordinated to the prevailing interest and trail along beside the latter for centuries afterwards. It follows from this that within a nation itself the individuals, even apart from their pecuniary circumstances, have quite different developments, and that an earlier interest, the peculiar form of intercourse of which has already been ousted by that belonging to a later interest, remains for a long time afterwards in possession of a traditional power in the illusory community (State, law), which has won an existence independent of the individuals; a power which in the last resort can only be broken by a revolution. This explains why, with reference to individual points which allow of a more general summing-up, consciousness can sometimes appear further advanced than the contemporary empirical relationships, so that in the struggles of a later epoch one can refer to earlier theoreticians as authorities.

On the other hand, in countries which, like North America, begin in an already advanced historical epoch, the development proceeds very rapidly. Such countries have no other natural premises than the individuals, who settled there and were led to do so because the forms of intercourse of the old countries did not correspond to their wants. Thus they begin with the most advanced individuals of the old countries, and, therefore, with the correspondingly most advanced form of intercourse, before this form of intercourse has been able to establish itself in the old countries. This is the case with all colonies, insofar as they are not mere military or trading stations. Carthage, the Greek colonies, and Iceland in the eleventh and twelfth centuries, provide examples of this. A similar relationship issues from conquest, when a form of intercourse which has evolved on another soil is brought over complete to the conquered country: whereas in its home it was still encumbered with interests and relationships left over from earlier periods, here it can and must be established completely and without hindrance, if only to assure the conquerors' lasting power. (England and Naples after the Norman conquest, when they received the most perfect form of feudal organisation.)

*   *   *

This contradiction between the productive forces and the form of intercourse, which, as we saw, has occurred several times in past history, without, however, endangering the basis, necessarily on each occasion burst out in a revolution, taking on at the same time various subsidiary forms, such as all-embracing collisions, collisions of various classes, contradiction of consciousness, battle of ideas, etc., political conflict, etc. From a narrow point of view one may isolate one of these subsidiary forms and consider it as the basis of these revolutions; and this is all the more easy as the individuals who started the revolutions had illusions about their own activity according to their degree of culture and the stage of historical development.

Thus all collisions in history have their origin, according to our view, in the contradiction between the productive forces and the form of intercourse. Incidentally, to lead to collisions in a country, this contradiction need not necessarily have reached its extreme limit in this particular country. The competition with industrially more advanced countries, brought about by the expansion of international intercourse, is sufficient to produce a similar contradiction in countries with a backward industry (e.g. the latent proletariat in Germany brought into view by view by the competition of English industry).

Conquest

This whole interpretation of history appears to be contradicted by the fact of conquest. Up till now violence, war, pillage, murder and robbery, etc. have been accepted as the driving force of history. Here we must limit ourselves to the chief points and take, therefore, only the most striking example—the destruction of an old civilisation by a barbarous people and the resulting formation of an entirely new organisation of society. (Rome and the barbarians; feudalism and Gaul; the Byzantine Empire and the Turks.)

With the conquering barbarian people war itself is still, as indicated above, a regular form of intercourse, which is the more eagerly exploited as the increase in population together with the traditional and, for it, the only possible, crude mode of production gives rise to the need for new means of production. In Italy, on the other hand, the concentration of landed property (caused not only by buying-up and indebtedness but also by inheritance, since loose living being rife and marriage rare, the old families gradually died out and their possessions fell into the hands of a few) and its conversion into grazing-land (caused not only by the usual economic forces still operative today but by the importation of plundered and tribute-corn and the resultant lack of demand for Italian corn) brought about the almost total disappearance of the free population. The very slaves died out again and again, and had constantly to be replaced by new ones. Slavery remained the basis of the whole productive system. The plebeians, midway between freemen and slaves, never succeeded in becoming more than a proletarian rabble. Rome indeed never became more than a city; its connection with the provinces was almost exclusively political and could, therefore, easily be broken again by political events.

Nothing is more common than the notion that in history up till now it has only been a question of *taking*. The barbarians *take* the Roman Empire, and this fact of taking is made to explain the transition from the old world to the feudal system. In this taking by barbarians, however, the question is, whether the nation which is conquered has evolved industrial productive forces, as is the case with modern peoples, or whether their productive forces are based for the most part merely on their association and on the community. Taking is further determined by the object taken. A banker's fortune, consisting of paper, cannot be taken at all, without the taker's submitting to the conditions of production and intercourse of the country taken. Similarly the total industrial capital of a modern industrial country. And finally, everywhere there is very soon an end to taking, and when there is nothing more to take, you have to set about producing. From this necessity of producing, which very soon asserts itself, it follows that the form of community adopted by the settling conquerors must correspond to the stage of development of the productive forces they find in existence; or, if this is not the case from the start, it must change according to the productive forces. By this, too, is explained the fact, which people profess to have noticed everywhere in the period following the migration of the peoples, namely, that the servant was master, and that the conquerors very soon took over language, culture and manners from the conquered. The feudal system was by no means brought complete from Germany, but had its origin, as far as the conquerors were concerned, in the martial organisation of the army during the actual conquest, and this only evolved after the conquest into the feudal system proper through the action of the productive forces found in the conquered countries. To what an extent this form was determined by the productive forces is shown by the abortive attempts to realise other forms derived from reminiscences of ancient Rome (Charlemagne, etc.).

Contradictions of Big Industry: Revolution

Our investigation hitherto started from the instruments of production, and it has already shown that private property was a necessity for certain industrial stages. In *industrie extractive* private property still coincides with labour; in small industry and all agriculture up till now property is the necessary consequence of the existing instruments of production; in big industry the contradiction between the instrument of production and private property appears from the first time and is the product of big industry; moreover, big industry must be highly developed to produce this contradiction. And thus only with big industry does the abolition of private property become possible.

In big industry and competition the whole mass of conditions of existence, limitations, biases of individuals, are fused together into the two simplest forms: private property and labour. With money every form of intercourse, and intercourse itself, is considered fortuitous for the individuals. Thus money implies that all previous intercourse was only intercourse of individuals under particular conditions, not of individuals as individuals. These conditions are reduced to two: accumulated labour or private property, and actual labour. If both or one of these ceases, then intercourse comes to a standstill. The modern economists themselves, e.g. Sismondi, Cherbuliez, etc., oppose "association of individuals" to "association of capital". On the other hand, the individuals themselves are entirely subordinated to the division of labour and hence are brought into the most complete dependence on one another. Private property, insofar as within labour itself it is opposed to labour, evolves out of the necessity of accumulation, and has still, to begin with, rather the form of the communality; but in its further development it approaches more and more the modern form of private property. The division of labour implies from the outset the division of the *conditions* of labour, of tools and materials, and thus the splitting-up of accumulated capital among different owners, and thus, also, the division between capital and labour, and the different forms of property itself. The more the division of labour develops and accumulation grows, the sharper are the forms that this process of differentiation assumes. Labour itself can only exist on the premise of this fragmentation.

Thus two facts are here revealed. First the productive forces appear as a world for themselves, quite independent of and divorced from the individuals, alongside the individuals: the reason for this is that the individuals, whose forces they are, exist split up and in opposition to one another, whilst, on the other hand, these forces are only real forces in the intercourse and association of these individuals. Thus, on the one hand, we have a totality of productive forces, which have, as it were, taken on a material form and are for the individuals no longer the forces of the individuals but of private property, and hence of the individuals only insofar as they are owners of private property themselves. Never, in any earlier period, have the productive forces taken on a form so indifferent to the intercourse of individuals *as* individuals, because their intercourse itself was formerly a restricted one. On the other hand, standing over against these productive forces, we have the majority of the individuals from whom these forces have been wrested away, and who, robbed thus of all real life-content, have become abstract individuals, but who are, however, only by this fact put into a position to enter into relation with one another *as individuals*.

The only connection which still links them with the productive forces and with their own existence—labour—has lost all semblance of self-activity and only sustains their life by stunting it. While in the earlier periods self-activity and the production of material life were separated, in that they devolved on different persons, and while, on account of the narrowness of the individuals themselves, the production of material life was considered as a subordinate mode of self-activity, they now diverge to such an extent that altogether material life appears as the end, and what produces this material life, labour (which is now the only possible but, as we see, negative form of self-activity), as the means.

Thus things have now come to such a pass that the individuals must appropriate the existing totality of productive forces, not only to achieve self-activity, but, also, merely to safeguard their very existence. This appropriation is first determined by the object to be appropriated, the productive forces, which have been developed to a totality and which only exist within a universal intercourse. From this aspect alone, therefore, this appropriation must have a universal character corresponding to the productive forces and the intercourse.

The appropriation of these forces is itself nothing more than the development of the individual capacities corresponding to the material instruments of production. The appropriation of a totality of instruments of production is, for this very reason, the development of a totality of capacities in the individuals themselves.

This appropriation is further determined by the persons appropriating. Only the proletarians of the present day, who are completely shut off from all self-activity, are in a position to achieve a complete and no longer restricted self-activity, which consists in the appropriation of a totality of productive forces and in the thus postulated development of a totality of capacities. All earlier revolutionary appropriations were restricted; individuals, whose self-activity was restricted by a crude instrument of production and a limited intercourse, appropriated this crude instrument of production, and hence merely achieved a new state of limitation. Their instrument of production became their property, but they themselves remained subordinate to the division of labour and their own instrument of production. In all expropriations up to now, a mass of individuals remained subservient to a single instrument of production; in the appropriation by the proletarians, a mass of instruments of production must be made subject to each individual, and property to all. Modern universal intercourse can be controlled by individuals, therefore, only when controlled by all.

This appropriation is further determined by the manner in which it must be effected. It can only be effected through a union, which by the character of the proletariat itself can again only be a universal one, and through a revolution, in which, on the one hand, the power of the earlier mode of production and intercourse and social organisation is overthrown, and, on the other hand, there develops the universal character and the energy of the proletariat, without which the revolution cannot be accomplished; and in which, further, the proletariat rids itself of everything that still clings to it from its previous position in society.

Only at this stage does self-activity coincide with material life, which corresponds to the development of individuals into complete individuals and the casting-off of all natural limitations. The transformation of labour into self-activity corresponds to the transformation of the earlier limited intercourse into the intercourse of individuals as such. With the appropriation of the total productive forces through united individuals, private property comes to an end. Whilst previously in history a particular condition always appeared as accidental, now the isolation of individuals and the particular private gain of each man have themselves become accidental.

The individuals, who are no longer subject to the division of labour, have been conceived by the philosophers as an ideal, under the name "Man". They have conceived the whole process which we have outlined as the evolutionary process of "Man", so that at every historical stage "Man" was substituted for the individuals and shown as the motive force of history. The whole process was thus conceived as a process of the self-estrangement of "Man", and this was essentially due to the fact that the average individual of the later stage was always foisted on to the earlier stage, and the consciousness of a later age on to the individuals of an earlier. Through this inversion, which from the first is an abstract image of the actual conditions, it was possible to transform the whole of history into an evolutionary process of consciousness.

Finally, from the conception of history we have sketched we obtain these further conclusions: (1) In the development of productive forces there comes a stage when productive forces and means of intercourse are brought into being, which, under the existing relationships, only cause mischief, and are no longer productive but destructive forces (machinery and money); and connected with this a class is called forth, which has to bear all the burdens of society without enjoying its advantages, which, ousted from society, is forced into the most decided antagonism to all other classes; a class which forms the majority of all members of society, and from which emanates the consciousness of the necessity of a fundamental revolution, the communist consciousness, which may, of course, arise among the other classes too through the contemplation of the situation of this class. (2) The conditions under which definite productive forces can be applied are the conditions of the rule of a definite class of society, whose social power, deriving from its property, has its *practical*-idealistic expression in each case in the form of the State; and, therefore, every revolutionary struggle is directed against a class, which till then has been in power.[1] (3) In all revolutions up till now the mode of activity always remained unscathed and it was only a question of a different distribution of this activity, a new distribution of labour to other persons, whilst the communist revolution is directed against the preceding *mode* of activity, does away with *labour*, and abolishes the rule of all classes with the classes themselves, because it is carried through by the class which no longer counts as a class in society, is not recognised as a class, and is in itself the expression of the dissolution of all classes, nationalities, etc. within present society; and (4) Both for the production on a mass scale of this communist consciousness, and for the success of the cause itself, the alternation of men on a mass scale is

---

[1] [Marginal note by Marx:] The people are interested in maintaining the present state of production.

necessary, an alteration which can only take place in a practical movement, a *revolution*; this revolution is necessary, therefore, not only
because the *ruling* class cannot be overthrown in any other way, but
also because the class *overthrowing* it can only in a revolution succeed
in ridding itself of all the muck of ages and become fitted to found
society anew.

SELECTIONS

FROM THE REMAINING PARTS OF THE GERMAN IDEOLOGY

(NOTE. The page references given are to the Complete Edition, Lawrence and Wishart, 1965.)

KANT AND LIBERALISM [p. 206]

The key to the criticism of liberalism advanced by Saint Max and his predecessors is the history of the German bourgeoisie. We shall put forward some aspects of this history since the French Revolution.

The state of Germany at the end of the last century is fully reflected in Kant's *Critik der practischen Vernunft*. While the French bourgeoisie, by means of the most colossal revolution that history has ever known, was achieving domination and conquering the Continent of Europe, while the already politically emancipated English bourgeoisie was revolutionising industry and subjugating India politically, and all the rest of the world commercially, the impotent German burghers did not get any further than "good will". Kant was satisfied with "good will" alone, even if it remained entirely without result, and he transferred the *realisation* of this good will, the harmony between it and the needs and impulses of individuals, to *the world beyond*. Kant's good will fully corresponds to the impotence, depression and wretchedness of the German burghers, whose petty interests were never capable of developing into the common, national interests of a class and who were, therefore, constantly exploited by the bourgeois of all other nations. These petty, local interests had as their counterpart, on the one hand, the truly local and provincial narrow-mindedness of the German burghers and, on the other hand, their cosmopolitan swollenheadedness. In general, from the time of the Reformation German development has borne a completely petty-bourgeois character. The old feudal aristocracy was, for the most part, annihilated in the peasant wars; what remained of it were either imperial petty princes who gradually achieved a certain independence for themselves and aped the absolute monarchy on a minute, small-town scale, or lesser landowners who, after squandering their little bit of property at the tiny courts, gained their livelihood from petty positions in the toy armies and government offices—or, finally, Junkers from the backwoods, who lived a life of which even the most modest English squire or French *gentilhomme de province* would have been ashamed. Agriculture was carried on by a method which was neither parcellation nor large-scale production, and which, despite the preservation of feudal dependence and corvées, never drove the peasants to seek emancipation, both because this very method of farming did not allow the emergence of any active revolutionary class and because of the absence of the revolutionary bourgeoisie corresponding to such a peasant class.

As regards the burghers, we can only emphasise here a few characteristic factors. It is characteristic that linen manufacture, i.e. an industry based on hand-spinning and the hand-weaving loom, came to be of some importance in Germany at the very time when in England those cumbersome tools were already being ousted by machines. Most characteristic of all is the position of the German burghers in relation to *Holland*. Holland, the only part of the Hanseatic League that became of commercial importance, tore itself free, cut Germany off from world trade except for two ports (Hamburg and Bremen) and since then dominated the whole of German trade. The German burghers were too impotent to set limits to exploitation by the Dutch. The bourgeoisie of little Holland, with its well-developed class interests, was more powerful than the numerically far greater German burghers with their indifference and their divided petty interests. Corresponding to the splitting up of interests, political organisation was also split up into the small principalities and the free imperial cities. How could *political* concentration arise in a country which lacked all the *economic* conditions for it? The impotence of each separate sphere of life (one cannot speak here of estates or classes, but at most only of former estates and classes not yet born) did not allow any one of them to gain exclusive domination. The inevitable consequence was that during the epoch of absolute monarchy, which was seen here in its most stunted, semi-patriarchal form, the special sphere which, owing to division of labour, was responsible for the work of administration of public interests acquired an abnormal independence, which became still greater in the bureaucracy of modern times.

Thus, the State built itself up into an apparently independent force, and this position, which in other countries was only transitory—a transition stage—it has maintained in Germany until the present day. It is this position of the State which explains both the honest character of the civil servant that is found nowhere else, and all the illusions about the State which are current in Germany, as well as the apparent independence of German theoreticians in relation to the burghers—the seeming contradiction between the form in which these theoreticians express the interest of the burghers and these interests themselves.

We find again in Kant the characteristic form which French liberalism, based on real class interests, assumed in Germany. Neither he, nor the German burghers, whose whitewashing spokesman he was, noticed that these theoretical ideas of the bourgeoisie had as their basis material interests and a *will* that was conditioned and determined by the material relations of production. Kant, therefore, separated this theoretical expression from the interests which it expressed; he made the materially motivated determinations of the will of the French bourgeois into *pure* self-determinations of *"free will"*, of the will in and for itself, of the human will, and so converted it into purely ideological conceptual determinations and moral postulates. Hence the German petty bourgeois recoiled in horror from the practice of this energetic bourgeois liberalism as soon as this practice showed itself, both in the Reign of Terror and in shameless bourgeois profit-making.

Under the rule of Napoleon, the German burghers pursued to an even greater degree their petty trade and their great illusions. As regards the petty-trading spirit which predominated in Germany at that time, Saint Sancho can, *inter alia*, compare Jean Paul, in order to quote works of fiction, the only sources accessible to him. The German burghers, who cursed Napoleon for compelling them to drink chicory and for disturbing their peace with military billeting and recruiting of conscripts, reserved all their moral indignation for Napoleon and all their admiration for England; yet Napoleon rendered them the greatest services by cleaning out Germany's Augean stables and establishing civilised means of communication, whereas England only waited for the opportunity to exploit them *à tort et à travers*. In the same petty-bourgeois spirit the German princes imagined they were fighting for the principle of legitimism and against revolution, whereas they were only the paid mercenaries of the English bourgeoisie. In the atmosphere of these universal illusions it was quite in the order of things that the estates privileged to cherish illusions—ideologists, school-masters, students, members of the *Tugendbund*[1]—should talk

[1] *Tugendbund (League of Virtue)*—political secret society which came into being in Prussia in 1808. Its aims included the kindling of the patriotic feelings of the population the fight for the liberation of Germany from the Napoleonic occupation and the establishment of a constitutional government. At Napoleon's request the King of Prussia formally dissolved the society in 1809, but it continued to exist until 1815.—*Ed.*

big and give a suitable high-flown expression to the universal mood of fantasy and indifference.

The July revolution—we mention only a few main points and therefore omit the intermediary stage—imposed on the Germans from outside the political forms corresponding to a developed bourgeoisie. Since German economic relations had by no means reached the level of development to which these political forms corresponded, the burghers accepted them merely as abstract ideas, principles valid in and for themselves, pious wishes and phrases, Kantian self-determinations of the will and of the people, such as they ought to be. Their attitude, therefore, to these forms was far more moral and disinterested than that of other nations, i.e. they exhibited a highly peculiar narrow-mindedness and remained unsuccessful in all their endeavours.

Finally, the ever more powerful development of foreign competition and world intercourse—from which it became less and less possible for Germany to stand aside—forced the scattered local interests of the Germans to unite into some sort of harmony. Particularly since 1840, the German burghers began to think about safeguarding these common interests; their attitude became national and liberal and they demanded protective tariffs and constitutions. Thus they have now got almost as far as the French bourgeoisie in 1789.

THE LANGUAGE OF PROPERTY [p. 245]

And then M. Destutt de Tracy undertakes to prove that *propriété*, *individualité* and *personalité* are identical, that the "Ego" (*moi*) also includes "mine" (*mein*), and he finds as a natural basis for property that

"nature has endowed man with an inevitable and inalienable property, property in the form of his own individuality". (p. 17. *Traité de la volonté*, Paris, 1826.). . . .

Having thus made private property and personality identical, Destutt de Tracy with a play on the words *propriété* and *propre* (One's own—*Ed.*), like Stirner with his play on the words *Mein* (Mine—*Ed.*) and *Meinung* (Opinion, view.—*Ed.*), *Eigentum* (Property—*Ed.*) and *Eigenheit* (Peculiarity—*Ed.*), arrives at the following conclusion:

"It is therefore, quite futile to argue about whether it would be better for none of us to have anything of our own. . . ." (p. 22). . . .

If, therefore, the bourgeois explains to the communists: by abolishing my existence *as a bourgeois*, you abolish my existence *as an individual*; if, therefore, he identifies himself as a bourgeois with himself as an individual, one must, at least, recognise his frankness and shamelessness. For the bourgeois it is actually the case, he believes himself to be an individual only insofar as he is a bourgeois.

As soon, however, as the theoreticians of the bourgeoisie come forward and give a general expression to this assertion, also theoretically identifying the property of the bourgeois with individuality and wanting to give a logical justification for this identification, then this nonsense begins to become solemn and holy.

Above "Stirner" refuted the communist abolition of private property by first transforming private property into "having" and then declaring the verb "to have" an indispensable word, an eternal truth, because even in communist society it could happen that Stirner will "have" a stomach-ache. In exactly the same way he here bases the impossibility of abolishing private property by transforming it into the concept of property ownership, by exploiting the etymological connection between the words *Eigentum* and *eigen*[1] and declaring the word *eigen* an eternal truth, because even under the communist system it could happen that a stomach-ache will be *eigen* to him. All this theoretical nonsense, which seeks refuge in etymology, would be impossible if the actual private property that the communists want to abolish had not been transformed into the abstract notion of "property". This transformation, on the one hand, saves one the trouble of having to say anything, or even merely to know anything, about actual private property and, on the other hand, makes it easy to discover a contradiction in communism, since *after* the abolition of (*actual*) property it is, of course, easy to discover still all sorts of things which can be included in the term "property". In reality, of course, the situation is just the reverse. In reality I possess private property only insofar as I have something vendible, whereas what is peculiar to me [*meine Eigenheit*] may not be vendible at all. My frock-coat is private property for me only so long as I can barter, pawn or sell it, so long [as it] is [marketable]. If it loses that feature, if it becomes tattered, it can still have a number of features which make it of value *to me*, it

[1] Own, peculiar.—*Ed.*

may even become a feature of me and turn me into a tatterdemalion. But no economist would think of classing it as my private property, since it does not enable me to command any, even the smallest, amount of other people's labour. A lawyer, an ideologist of private property, could perhaps still indulge in such twaddle. Private property alienates the individuality not only of people but also of things. Land has nothing to do with rent of land, the machine has nothing to do with profit. For the landed proprietor, land has the significance only of rent of land; he leases his plots of land and receives rent; this is a feature which land can lose without losing one single inherent feature, without, for example, losing any part of its fertility; it is a feature the extent and even the existence of which depends on social relations which are created and destroyed without the assistance of individual landed proprietors. It is the same with machines. How little connection there is between money, the most general form of property, and personal peculiarity, how much they are directly opposed to each other was already known to Shakespeare better than to our theorising petty bourgeois:

Thus much of this will make black, white; foul, fair;
Wrong, right; base, noble; old, young; coward, valiant.
This yellow slave. . .
Will make the hoar leprosy adored. . .
                                        This it is
That makes the wappened widow wed again;
She, whom the spital-house and ulcerous sores
Would cast the gorge at, this embalms and spices
To th' April day again. . .
                                        Thou visible god,
That solder'st close impossibilities,
And makest them kiss!

In a word, rent of land, profit, etc., these actual forms of existence of private property, are *social relations* corresponding to a definite stage of production, and they are "*individual*" only so long as they have not become fetters on the existing productive forces. . . .

For the bourgeois it is so much the easier to prove on the basis of his language, the identity of commercial and individual, or even universal, human relations, since this language itself is a product of the bourgeoisie, and therefore in actuality as in language the relations of buying and selling have been made the basis of all others. For example, *propriété*—property [*Eigentum*] and feature [*Eigenschaft*]; property—possession [*Eigentum*] and peculiarity [*Eigentümlichkeit*]; "*eigen*" ["one's own"]—in the commercial and in the individual sense; *valeur*, value, *Wert*;[1] commerce, *Verkehr*;[2] *échange*, exchange, *Austausch*,[3] etc., all of which are used both for commerical relations and for features and mutual relations of individuals as such. In the other modern languages this is equally the case.

PHILOSOPHY AND REALITY [p. 254]

This path [to the materialistic outlook] was already indicated in the *Deutsch-Französische Jahrbücher*—in the *Einleitung zur Kritik der Hegelschen Rechtsphilosophie* and *Zur Judenfrage*. But since at that time this was done in philosophical phraseology, the traditionally occurring philosophical expressions such as "human essence", "genus", etc. gave the German theoreticians the desired excuse for misunderstanding the real trend of thought and believing that here again it was a question merely of giving a new turn to their worn-out theoretical garments. . . . One has to "leave philosophy aside" (Wigand, p. 187, cf. Hess, *Die letzten Philosophen*, p. 8), one has to leap out of it and devote oneself like an ordinary man to the study of actuality, for which there exists also an enormous amount of literary material, unknown, of course, to the philosophers. . . . Philosophy and the study of the actual world have the same relation to one another as masturbation and sexual love.

PERSONAL, VERSUS GENERAL, INTERESTS [p. 265]

How is it that personal interests always develop, against the will of individuals, into class interests, into common interests which acquire independent existence in relation to the individual persons, and in their independence assume the form of *general* interests? How is it that as such they come into contradiction with actual individuals and in this contradiction, by which they are defined as *general* interests, they can

---

[1] Worth, value.—*Ed.*
[2] Intercourse, traffic, commerce, communication.—*Ed.*
[3] Exchange, barter, interchange.—*Ed.*

be conceived by consciousness as *ideal* and even as religious, holy interests? How is it that in this process of private interests acquiring independent existence as class interests the personal behaviour of the individual is bound to undergo substantiation, alienation, and at the same time exists as a power independent of him and without him, created by intercourse, and becomes transformed into social relations, into a series of powers which determine and subordinate the individual, and which, therefore, appear in the imagination as "holy" powers? If Sancho [Stirner] had only understood the fact that within the frameworks of definite *modes of production*, which, of course, are not dependent on the will, alien practical forces, which are independent not only of isolated individuals but even of all of them together, always come to stand above people—then he could be fairly indifferent as to whether this fact is presented in a religious form or distorted in the imagination of the egoist, for whom everything occurs in the imagination, in such a way that he puts nothing above himself. Sancho would then have descended from the realm of speculation into the realm of reality, from what people imagine they are to what they actually are, from what they imagine about themselves to how they act and are bound to act in definite circumstances. What seems to him a product of *thought*, he would have understood to be a product of life. . . .

Incidentally, even in the banal, petty-bourgeois German form in which Sancho perceives the contradiction of personal and general interests, he should have realised that individuals have always started out from themselves, and could not do otherwise, and that therefore both the aspects he noted are aspects of the personal development of individuals; both are equally engendered by the empirical conditions of life, both are only expressions of *one and the same* personal development of people and are therefore only in *seeming* contradiction to each other. . . .

Communism is simply incomprehensible to our saint because the communists do not put egoism against self-sacrifice or self-sacrifice against egoism, nor do they express this contradiction theoretically either in its sentimental or in its highflown ideological form; on the contrary, they demonstrate the material basis engendering it, with which it disappears of itself. The communists do not preach *morality* at all, such as Stirner preaches so extensively. They do not put to people the moral demand: love one another, do not be egoists, etc.; on the contrary, they are very well aware that egoism, just as much as self-sacrifice, *is* in definite circumstances a necessary form of the self-assertion of individuals. Hence, the communists by no means want . . . to do away with the "private individual" for the sake of the "general", self-sacrificing man. . . .

Theoretical communists, the only ones who have time to devote to the study of history, are distinguished precisely because they alone have *discovered* that throughout history the "general interest" is created by individuals who are defined as "private persons". They know that this contradiction is only a *seeming* one because one side of it, the so-called "general", is constantly being produced by the other side, private interest, and by no means opposes the latter as an independent force with an independent history—so that this contradiction is in practice always being destroyed and reproduced. Hence it is not a question of the Hegelian "negative unity" of two sides of a contradiction, but of the materially determined destruction of the preceding materially determined mode of life of individuals, with the disappearance of which this contradiction together with its unity also disappears.

ONE-SIDED DEVELOPMENT [p. 284]

If the circumstances in which the individual lives allow him only the [one]-sided development of a single quality at the expense of all the rest, if they give him the material and time to develop only that one quality, then this individual achieves only a one-sided, crippled development. No moral preaching avails here. And the manner in which this one, preferentially favoured quality develops depends again, on the one hand, on the material available for its development and, on the other hand, on the degree and manner in which the other qualities are suppressed. . . .

In the case of an individual, for example, whose life embraces a wide circle of varied activities and practical relations to the world, and who, therefore, lives a many-sided life, thought has the same character of universality as every other manifestation of his life. Consequently, it neither becomes fixed in the form of abstract thought nor does it need complicated tricks of reflection when the individual passes from thought to some other manifestation of life. From the outset it is always a factor in the total life of the individual, one which disappears and is reproduced as *required*. . . .

The fact that under favourable circumstances some individuals are able to rid themselves of their local narrow-mindedness is not at all because the individuals by their reflection imagine that they have got rid of, or intend to get rid of, this local narrow-mindedness, but because they, in their empirical reality, and owing to empirical needs, have been able to bring about world intercourse.

WILL AS THE BASIS OF RIGHT [p. 357]

In actual history, those theoreticians who regarded *power* as the basis of right, were in direct contradiction to those who looked on *will* as the basis of right. . . . If power is taken as the basis of right, as Hobbes, etc. do, then right, law, etc. are merely the symptom, the expression of *other* relations upon which State power rests. The material life of individuals, which by no means depends merely on their "will", their mode of production and form of intercourse, which mutually determine each other—this is the real basis of the State and remains so at all the stages at which division of labour and private property are still necessary, quite independently of the *will* of individuals. These actual relations are in no way created by the State power; on the contrary they are the power creating it. The individuals who rule in these conditions, besides having to constitute their power in the form of the *State*, have to give their will, which is determined by these definite conditions, a universal expression as the will of the State, as law—an expression whose content is always determined by the relations of this class, as the civil and criminal law demonstrates in the clearest possible way. . . . Their personal power is based on conditions of life which as they develop are common to many individuals, and the continuance of which they, as ruling individuals, have to maintain against others and, at the same time, maintain they hold good for all. The expression of this will, which is determined by their common interests, is law. It is precisely because individuals who are independent of one another assert themselves and their own will, which on this basis is inevitably egoistical in their mutual relations, that self-denial is made necessary in law and right, self-denial in the exceptional case, and self-assertion of their interests in the average case (which, therefore, not *they*, but only the "egoist in agreement with himself" regards as self-denial). The same applies to the classes which are ruled, whose will plays just as small a part in determining the existence of law and the State. For example, so long as the productive forces are still insufficiently developed to make competition superfluous, and therefore would give rise to competition over and over again, for so long the classes which are ruled would be wanting the impossible if they had the "will" to abolish competition and with it the State and the law. Incidentally, too, it is only in the imagination of the ideologist that this "will" arises before conditions have developed far enough to make its production possible. After conditions have developed sufficiently to produce it, the ideologist is able to imagine this will as being purely arbitrary and therefore as conceivable at all times and under all circumstances.

Like right, so crime, i.e. the struggle of the isolated individual against the prevailing conditions, is not the result of pure arbitrariness. On the contrary, it depends on the same conditions as that rule. The same visionaries who see in right and law the domination of some independently existing, general will can see in crime the mere violation of right and law. Hence the State does not exist owing to the ruling will, but the State which arises from the material mode of life of individuals has also the form of a ruling will. If the latter loses its domination, it means that not only has the will changed but also the material existence and life of the individuals, and only for that reason has their will changed. It is possible for rights and laws to be "inherited", but in that case they are no longer ruling, but nominal, of which striking examples are furnished by the history of ancient Roman law and English law. We saw earlier how a theory and history of pure thought could arise among philosophers owing to the divorce between ideas and the individuals and their empirical relations which serve as the basis of these ideas. In the same way, here too one can divorce right from its real basis, whereby one obtains a "ruling will" which in different epochs becomes modified in various ways and has its own, independent history in its creations, the laws. On this account, political and civil history becomes ideologically merged in a history of the rule of successive laws. This is the specific illusion of lawyers and politicians. . . .

ARTISTIC TALENT [p. 430]

He [Stirner] imagines that the so-called organisers of labour[1] wanted to organise the entire activity of each individual, and yet it is precisely among them that a difference is drawn between directly productive labour, which has to be organised, and labour which is not directly productive. In regard to the latter, however, it was not their view, as Sancho imagines, that each should do the work of Raphael, but that anyone in whom there is a potential Raphael should be able to develop without hindrance. Sancho imagines that Raphael produced his pictures independently of the division of labour that existed in Rome at the time. If he were to compare Raphael with Leonardo da Vinci and Titian, he would know how greatly Raphael's works of art depended on the flourishing of Rome at that time, which occurred under Florentine influence, while the works of Leonardo depended on the state of things in Florence, and the works of Titian, at a later period, depended on the totally different development of Venice. Raphael as much as any other artist was determined by the technical advances in art made before him, by the organisation of society and the division of labour in his locality, and, finally, by the division of labour in all the countries with which his locality had intercourse. Whether an individual like Raphael succeeds in developing his talent depends wholly on demand, which in turn depends on the division of labour and the conditions of human culture resulting from it.

In proclaiming the uniqueness of work in science and art, Stirner adopts a position far inferior to that of the bourgeoisie. At the present time it has already been found necessary to organise this "unique" activity. Horace Vernet would not have had time to paint even a tenth of his pictures if he regarded them as works which "only this Unique person is capable of producing". In Paris, the great demand for vaudevilles and novels brought about the organisation of work for their production, organisation which at any rate yields something better than its "unique" competitors in Germany. In astronomy, people like Arago, Herschel, Encke and Bessel considered it necessary to organise joint observations and only after that obtained some fruitful results. In historical science, it is absolutely impossible for the "Unique"

[1] *Organisers of labour*—utopian socialists (in particular Fourier and his followers) who put forward a utopian plan for transforming society through reforms, by means of the so-called "organisation of labour" which they opposed to the anarchy of production under capitalism.

to achieve anything at all, and in this field, too, the French long ago surpassed all other nations thanks to organisation of labour. Incidentally, it is self-evident that all these organisations based on modern division of labour still lead only to extremely limited results, representing a step forward only compared with the previous narrow isolation. . . .

The exclusive concentration of artistic talent in particular individuals, and its suppression in the broad mass which is bound up with this, is a consequence of division of labour. If, even in certain social conditions, everyone was an excellent painter, that would not at all exclude the possibility of each of them being also an original painter, so that here too the difference between "human" and "unique" labour amounts to sheer nonsense. In any case, with a communist organisation of society, there disappears the subordination of the artist to local and national narrowness, which arises entirely from division of labour, and also the subordination of the artist to some definite art, thanks to which he is exclusively a painter, sculptor, etc., the very name of his activity adequately expressing the narrowness of his professional development and his dependence on division of labour. In a communist society there are no painters but at most people who engage in painting among other activities.

UTILITARIANISM [p. 448]

Hegel has already proved in his *Phänomenologie* how this theory of mutual exploitation, which Bentham expounded *ad nauseum*, could already at the beginning of the present century have been considered a phase of the previous one. Look at his chapter on "The Struggle of Enlightenment with Superstition", where the theory of usefulness is depicted as the final result of enlightenment. The apparent stupidity of merging all the manifold relationships of people in the *one* relation of usefulness, this apparently metaphysical abstraction arises from the fact that, in modern bourgeois society, all relations are subordinated in practice to the one abstract monetary-commercial relation. This theory came to the fore with Hobbes and Locke at the same time as the first and second English revolutions, those first battles by which the bourgeoisie won political power. It is to be found even earlier, of course, among writers on political economy, as a tacit premise.

Political economy is the real science of this theory of utility; it acquires its true content among the Physiocrats, since they were the first to treat political economy systematically. In Helvétius and Holbach one can already find an idealisation of this doctrine, which fully corresponds to the attitude of opposition adopted by the French bourgeoisie before the revolution. In Holbach, all the activity of individuals in their mutual intercourse, e.g. speech, love, etc., is depicted as a relation of utility and utilisation. Hence the actual relations that are presupposed here are speech, love, the definite manifestations of definite qualities of individuals. Now these relations are supposed not to have the meaning *peculiar* to them but to be the expression and manifestation of some third relation introduced in their place, the *relation of utility or utilisation*. This *paraphrasing* ceases to be meaningless and arbitrary only when these relations have validity for the individual not on their own account, not as self-activity, but rather as disguises, though by no means disguises of the category of utilisation, but of an actual third aim and relation which is called the relation of utility.

The verbal masquerade only has meaning when it is the unconscious or deliberate expression of an actual masquerade. In this case, the utility relation has a quite definite meaning, namely, that I derive benefit for myself by doing harm to someone else (*exploitation de l'homme par l'homme*); further, in this case the use that I derive from some relation is in general alien to this relation, just as we saw above in connection with ability [*Vermögen*] that from each ability a product alien to it was demanded, a relation determined by social relations—and this is precisely the relation of utility.

All this is actually the case with the bourgeois. For him only *one* relation is valid on its own account—the relation of exploitation; all other relations have validity for him only insofar as he can include them under this one relation, and even where he encounters relations which cannot be directly subordinated to the relation of exploitation, he does at least subordinate them to it in his imagination. The material expression of this use is money, the representative of the value of all things, people and social relations. Incidentally, one sees at a glance that the category of "utilisation" is first of all abstracted from the actual relations of intercourse which I have with other people (but by no means from reflection and mere will) and then these relations are made out to be the reality of the category that has been abstracted from them themselves, a wholly metaphysical method of procedure. In exactly the same way and with the same justification, Hegel depicted all relations as relations of the objective spirit. Hence Holbach's theory is the historically justified philosophical illusion about the bourgeoisie just then developing in France, whose thirst for exploitation could still be described as a thirst for the full development of individuals in conditions of intercourse freed from the old feudal fetters. Liberation from the standpoint of the bourgeoisie, i.e. competition, was, of course, for the eighteenth century the only possible way of offering the individuals a new career for freer development. The theoretical proclamation of the consciousness corresponding to this bourgeois practice, the consciousness of mutual exploitation as the universal mutual relation of all individuals, was also a bold and open step forward, a mundane *enlightenment* as to the meaning of the political, patriarchal, religious and sentimental embroidery of exploitation under feudalism, an embroidery which corresponded to the form of exploitation at that time and which was made into a system especially by the theoretical writers of the absolute monarchy. . . .

The advances made by the theory of utility and exploitation, its various phases, are closely connected with the various periods of development of the bourgeoisie. In the case of Helvétius and Holbach, the actual content of the theory never went much beyond paraphrasing the mode of expression of the writers at the time of the absolute monarchy. With them it was a different method of expression; it reflected not so much the actual fact but rather the desire to reduce all relations to the relation of exploitation, and to explain the intercourse of people from material needs and the ways of satisfying them. The problem was set. Hobbes and Locke had before their eyes both the earlier development of the Dutch bourgeoisie (both of them had lived for some time in Holland) and the first political actions by which the English bourgeoisie emerged from local and provincial limitations, as well as a comparatively highly developed stage of manufacture, overseas trade and colonisation. This particularly applies to Locke, who wrote during the first period of English economy, at the time of the rise of joint-stock companies, the Bank of England and England's mastery of the seas. In their case, and particularly in that of Locke, the theory of exploitation was still directly connected with the economic content.

Helvétius and Holbach were confronted not only by English theory and the preceding development of the Dutch and English bourgeoisie, but also by the French bourgeoisie which was still struggling for its free development. The commercial spirit, universal in the eighteenth century, had especially in France taken possession of all classes in the form of speculation. The financial difficulties of the government and the resulting disputes over taxation occupied the attention of all France even at that time. In addition, Paris in the eighteenth century was the only world city, the only city where there was personal intercourse among individuals of all nations. These premises, combined with the more universal character typical of Frenchmen in general, gave the theory of Helvétius and Holbach its peculiar universal colouring, but at the same time deprived it of the positive economic content that was still to be found among the English. The theory which for the English still was simply the registration of a fact becomes for the French a philosophical system. This generality devoid of positive content, such as we find it in Helvétius and Holbach, is essentially different from the substantial comprehensive view which is first found in Bentham and Mill. The former corresponds to the struggling, still undeveloped bourgeoisie, the latter to the ruling, developed bourgeoisie.

The content of the theory of exploitation that was neglected by Helvétius and Holbach was developed and systematised by the Physiocrats—who worked at the same time as Holbach; but as they took as their basis the undeveloped economic relations of France where feudalism, under which landownership plays the chief role, was still not broken, they remained in thrall to the feudal outlook insofar as they declared landownership and land cultivation to be that [productive force] which determines the whole structure of society.

The theory of exploitation owes its further development in England to Godwin, and especially to Bentham, who gradually re-incorporated the economic content which the French had neglected, in proportion as the bourgeoisie succeeded in asserting itself both in England and in France. Godwin's *Political Justice* was written during the terror, and Bentham's chief works during and after the French Revolution and the development of large-scale industry in England. The complete union of the theory of utility with political economy is to be found, finally, in Mill.

At an earlier period political economy had been the subject of inquiry either by financiers, bankers and merchants, i.e. in general by persons directly concerned with economic relations, or by persons with an all-round education like Hobbes, Locke and Hume, for whom it was of importance as a branch of encyclopaedic knowledge. Thanks to the Physiocrats, political economy for the first time was raised to the rank of a special science and has been treated as such ever since. As a special branch of science it absorbed the other relations—political, juridical, etc.—to such an extent that it reduced them to economic relations. But it considered this subordination of all relations to itself only one aspect of these relations, and thereby allowed them for the rest an independent significance also outside political economy. The complete subordination of all existing relations to the relation of utility, and its unconditional elevation to be the sole content of all other relations, we find for the first time in Bentham, where, after the French Revolution and the development of large-scale industry, the bourgeoisie no longer appears as a special class, but as the class whose conditions of existence are those of the whole society.

When the sentimental and moral paraphrases, which for the French were the entire content of the utility theory, had been exhausted, all that remained for its further development was the question how individuals and relations were to be used, to be exploited. Meanwhile the reply to this question had already been given in political economy; the only possible step forward was by inclusion of the economic content. Bentham achieved this advance. But the idea had already been stated in political economy that the chief relations of exploitation are determined by production by and large, independently of the will of individuals who find them already in existence. Hence, no other field of speculative thought remained for the utility theory than the attitude of individuals to these important relations, the private exploitation of an already existing world by individuals. On this subject Bentham and his school indulged in lengthy moral reflections. Thereby the whole criticism of the existing world provided by the utility theory also moved within a narrow compass. Prejudiced in favour of the conditions of the bourgeoisie, it could criticise only those relations which had been handed down from a past epoch and were an obstacle to the development of the bourgeoisie. Hence, although the utility theory does expound the connection of all existing relations with economic relations it does so only in a restricted way.

From the outset the utility theory had the aspect of a theory of general utility, yet this aspect only became fraught with meaning when economic relations, especially division of labour and exchange, were included. With division of labour, the private activity of the individual becomes generally useful; Bentham's general utility becomes reduced to the same general utility that is operative in competition. By taking into account the economic relations of rent, profit and wages, the definite exploitation relations of separate classes were introduced, since the manner of exploitation depends on the position in life of the exploiter. Up to this point the theory of utility was able to base itself on definite social facts; its further account of the manner of exploitation amounts to a mere recital of catechism phrases.

The economic content gradually turned the utility theory into a mere apologia for the existing state of affairs, an attempt to prove that under existing conditions the mutual relations of people today are the most advantageous and generally useful. It has this character among all modern economists.

THE PHILOSOPHY OF ENJOYMENT [p. 458]

The *philosophy* which preaches enjoyment is as old in Europe as the Cyrenaic school. Just as in antiquity it was the *Greeks* who were the protagonists of this philosophy, so in modern times it is the *French*, and indeed on the same grounds, because their temperament and their society made them most capable of enjoyment. The philosophy of enjoyment was never anything but the ingenious language of certain social circles who had the privilege of enjoyment. Apart from the fact that the manner and content of their enjoyment was always determined by the whole structure of the rest of society and suffered from all its contradictions, this philosophy became a mere *phrase*, as soon as it began to lay claim to a universal character and proclaimed itself the outlook on life of society as a whole. It sank then to the level of edifying moralising, to a sophistical embellishment of existing society, or it was transformed into its opposite, by declaring compulsory asceticism to be enjoyment.

In modern times the philosophy of enjoyment arose with the decline of feudalism and with the transformation of the feudal landed nobility into the jovial, extravagant nobles of the court under the absolute monarchy. Among these nobles this philosophy has still to a great extent the form of a direct, naïve outlook on life which finds expression in memoirs, poems, novels, etc. It only becomes a real philosophy in the hands of a few writers of the revolutionary bourgeoisie, who, on the one hand, participated in the culture and mode of life of the court nobility and who, on the other hand, shared the more general outlook of the bourgeoisie, based on the more general conditions of existence of this class. It was, therefore, accepted by both classes, although from totally different points of view. Whereas among the nobility this language was restricted exclusively to the highest estate and to the conditions of life of this estate, it was given a generalised character by the bourgeoisie and applied to every individual without distinction, thus it was divorced from the conditions of life of these individuals. Thereby the theory of enjoyment was converted into an insipid and hypocritical moral doctrine. When, in the course of further development, the nobility was overthrown and the bourgeoisie brought into conflict with their opposite, the proletariat, the nobility became devoutly religious, and the bourgeoisie solemnly moral and strict in their theories, or else they succumbed to the above-mentioned hypocrisy, although the nobility in practice by no means renounced enjoyment, while among the bourgeoisie enjoyment even assumed an official, economic form—that of *luxury*.

The connection of the enjoyment of the individuals at any particular time with the class relations in which they live, and the conditions of production and intercourse which give rise to these relations, the narrowness of the hitherto existing forms of enjoyment which were outside the actual content of the life of people and in contradiction to it, the connection of every philosophy of enjoyment with the enjoyment actually present and the hypocrisy of such a philosophy when applied to all individuals without distinction—all this, of course, could only be discovered when it became possible to criticise the conditions of production and intercourse in the hitherto existing world, i.e. when the contradiction between the bourgeoisie and proletariat had given rise to communist and socialist outlooks. That shattered the basis of all morality, whether the morality of asceticism or of enjoyment.

NEEDS AND CONDITIONS [p. 474]

He [Stirner] imagines that people up to now have always formed a concept of man, and then won freedom for themselves to the extent that was necessary to realise this concept; that the measure of freedom that they achieved was determined each time by their idea of the ideal of man at the time. . . .

In reality, of course, what happened was that people won freedom for themselves each time to the extent that was dictated and permitted not by their ideal of man, but by the existing productive forces. All conquests of freedom hitherto, however, have been based on restricted productive forces. The production which these productive forces could provide was insufficient for the whole of society and made development possible only if some persons satisfied their needs at the expense of others, and therefore some—the minority—obtained the monopoly of development, while others—the majority—owing to the constant struggle to satisfy their most essential needs, were for the time being (i.e. until the birth of new revolutionary productive forces) excluded from any development. Thus, society has hitherto always developed within the framework of a contradiction—in antiquity the contradiction between free men and slaves, in the Middle Ages that between nobility and serfs, in modern times that between the bourgeoisie and the proletariat. This explains, on the one hand, the abnormal, "inhuman", means with which the oppressed class satisfies its needs, and, on the other hand, the narrow limits within which intercourse, and with it the whole ruling class, develops. Hence this restricted character of development consists not only in the exclusion of one class from development, but also in the narrow-mindedness of the excluding class, and the "inhuman" is to be found also within the ruling class. This so-called "inhuman" is just as much a product of present-day conditions as the "human" is; it is their negative aspect, the rebellion—which is not based on any new revolutionary productive force—against the prevailing conditions brought about by the existing productive forces, and against the way of satisfying needs that corresponds to these conditions. The positive expression "human" corresponds to the definite conditions *predominant* at a certain stage of production and to the way of satisfying needs determined by them, just as the negative expression "inhuman" corresponds to the attempt, within the existing mode of production, to negate these predominant conditions and the way of satisfying needs prevailing under them, an attempt that this stage of production daily engenders afresh.

———————

THE FREE DEVELOPMENT OF INDIVIDUALS [p. 482]

The transformation of the individual relationship into its opposite, a merely material relationship, the distinction of individuality and chance by the individuals themselves, as we have already shown, is an historical process and at different stages of development assumes different, ever sharper and more universal forms. In the present epoch, the domination of material conditions over individuals, and the suppression of individuality by chance, has assumed its sharpest and most universal form, thereby setting existing individuals a very definite task. It has set them the task of replacing the domination of circumstances and of chance over individuals by the domination of individuals over chance and circumstances. It has not, as Sancho imagines, put forward the demand that "I should develop myself", which up to now every individual has done without Sancho's good advice; it has instead called for liberation from one quite definite mode of development. This task, dictated by present-day conditions, coincides with the task of the communist organisation of society.

We have already shown above that the abolition of a state of things in which relationships become independent of individuals, in which individuality is subservient to chance and the personal relationships of individuals are subordinated to general class relationships, etc.— the abolition of this state of things is determined in the final analysis by the abolition of division of labour. We have also shown that the abolition of division of labour is determined by the development of intercourse and productive forces to such a degree of universality that private property and division of labour become fetters on them. We have further shown that private property can be abolished only on condition of an all-round development of individuals, because the existing character of intercourse and productive forces is an all-round one, and only individuals that are developing in an all-round fashion can appropriate them, i.e. can turn them into free manifestations of their lives. We have shown that at the present time individuals *must* abolish private property, because the productive forces and forms of intercourse have developed so far that, under the domination of private property, they have become destructive forces, and because the contradiction between the classes has reached its extreme limit. Finally, we have shown that the abolition of private property and of the division of labour is itself the union of individuals on the basis created by modern productive forces and world intercourse.

Within communist society, the only society in which the original and free development of individuals ceases to be a mere phrase, this development is determined precisely by the connection of individuals, a connection which consists partly in the economic prerequisites and partly in the necessary solidarity of the free development of all, and, finally, in the universal character of the activity of individuals on the basis of the existing productive forces. Here, therefore, the matter concerns individuals at a definite historical stage of development and by no means merely individuals chosen at random, even disregarding the indispensable communist revolution which itself is a general condition of their free development. The individuals' consciousness of their mutual relations will, of course, likewise become something quite different, and, therefore, will no more be the "principle of love" or *dévoument*, than it will be egoism.

LANGUAGE AND THOUGHT [p. 491]

For philosophers, one of the most difficult tasks is to descend from the world of thought to the actual world. *Language* is the immediate actuality of thought. Just as philosophers have given thought an independent existence, so they had to make language into an independent realm. This is the secret of philosophical language, in which thoughts in the form of words have their own content. The problem of descending from the world of thoughts to the actual world is turned into the problem of descending from language to life.

We have shown that thoughts and ideas acquire an independent existence in consequence of the personal circumstances and relations of individuals acquiring independent existence. We have shown that exclusive, systematic occupation with these thoughts on the part of ideologists and philosophers, and hence the systematisation of these thoughts, is a consequence of division of labour, and that, in particular, German philosophy is a consequence of German petty-bourgeois conditions. The philosophers would only have to dissolve their language into the ordinary language, from which it is abstracted, to recognise it as the distorted language of the actual world, and to realise that neither thoughts nor language in themselves form a realm of their own, that they are only *manifestations* of actual life.

"TRUE" SOCIALISM [p. 501]

The relation between German socialism and the proletarian movement in France and England is the same as that which we found in the first volume (cf. "Saint Max", "Political Liberalism") between German liberalism, as it has hitherto existed, and the movement of the French and English bourgeoisie. Alongside the German communists, a number of writers have appeared who have absorbed a few French and English communist ideas and amalgamated them with their own German philosophical premises. These "socialists" or "true socialists", as they call themselves, consider foreign communist literature not as the expression and the product of a real movement but as purely theoretical writings which have been evolved—in the same way as they imagine the German philosophical systems to have been evolved—by a process of "pure thought". It never occurs to them that, even when these writings do preach a system, they spring from the practical needs, the whole conditions of life of a particular class in particular countries. They innocently take on trust the illusion, cherished by some of these literary party representatives, that they are concerned with the "most reasonable" social order instead of with the needs of a particular class and time. . . . And what is the "*truth*" which they impart to socialism and communism? Since they find the ideas contained in socialist and communist literature quite unintelligible—partly by reason of their ignorance even of the literary connections, partly on account of their above-mentioned misunderstanding of socialist and communist literature—they attempt to clarify them by invoking the German ideology and notably that of Hegel and Feuerbach. They detach the communist systems, critical and polemical writings from the real movement, of which they are but the expression, and force them into an arbitrary connection with German philosophy. They detach the consciousness of certain historically conditioned spheres of life from these spheres and evaluate it in terms of true, absolute, i.e. German philosophical consciousness. With perfect consistency they transform the relations of these particular individuals into relations of "Man"; they interpret the thoughts of these particular individuals concerning their own relations as thoughts about "Man". In so doing, they have abandoned the realm of real history and returned to the realm of ideology, and since they are ignorant of the real connection, they can without difficulty fabricate some fantastic relationship with the help of the "absolute" or some other ideological method. This translation of

French ideas into the language of the German ideologists and this arbitrarily constructed relationship between communism and German ideology, then, constitute so-called "true socialism" ... true socialism, concerned no longer with real human beings but with "Man", has lost all revolutionary enthusiasm and proclaims instead the universal love of mankind. It turns as a result not to the proletarians but to the two most numerous classes of men in Germany, to the petty bourgeoisie with its philanthropic illusions and to the ideologists of this very same petty bourgeoisie. . . .The lack of any *real*, passionate, practical party conflict in Germany meant that even the social movement was at first a *merely* literary one. True socialism is a perfect example of a social literary movement that has come into being without any real party interests and now, after the formation of the communist party, it intends to persist in its despite.

SUPPLEMENTARY TEXTS

Karl Marx

THESES ON FEUERBACH

I

The chief defect of all hitherto existing materialism (that of Feuerbach included) is that the thing, reality, sensuousness, is conceived only in the form of the *object or of contemplation*, but not as *sensuous human activity*, *practice*, not subjectively. Hence, in contradistinction to materialism, the *active* side was developed abstractly by idealism—which, of course, does not know real, sensuous activity as such. Feuerbach wants sensuous objects, really distinct from the thought objects, but he does not conceive human activity itself as *objective* activity. Hence, in *Das Wesen des Christenthums*, he regards the theoretical attitude as the only genuinely human attitude, while practice is conceived and fixed only in its dirty-judaical manifestation. Hence he does not grasp the significance of "revolutionary", of "practical-critical", activity.

II

The question whether objective truth can be attributed to human thinking is not a question of theory but is a *practical question*. Man must prove the truth, i.e. the reality and power, the this-sidedness of his thinking in practice. The dispute over the reality or non-reality of thinking that is isolated from practice is a purely *scholastic* question.

III

The materialist doctrine concerning the changing of circumstances and upbringing forgets that circumstances are changed by men and that it is essential to educate the educator himself. This doctrine must, therefore, divide society into two parts, one of which is superior to society.

The coincidence of the changing of circumstances and of human activity or self-changing can be conceived and rationally understood only as *revolutionary practice*.

IV

Feuerbach starts out from the fact of religious self-alienation, of the duplication of the world into a religious world and a secular one. His work consists in resolving the religious world into its secular basis. But that the secular basis detaches itself from itself and establishes itself as an independent realm in the clouds can only be explained by the cleavages and self-contradictions within this secular basis. The latter must, therefore, in itself be both understood in its contradiction and revolutionised in practice. Thus, for instance, after the earthly family is discovered to be the secret of the holy family, the former must then itself be destroyed in theory and in practice.

V

Feuerbach, not satisfied with *abstract thinking*, wants *contemplation*; but he does not conceive sensuousness as *practical*, human-sensuous activity.

VI

Feuerbach resolves the religious essence into the *human* essence. But the human essence is no abstraction inherent in each single individual. In its reality it is the ensemble of the social relations.

Feuerbach, who does not enter upon a criticism of this real essence, is consequently compelled:

1. To abstract from the historical process and to fix the religious sentiment as something by itself and to presuppose an abstract—*isolated*—human individual.

2. Essence, therefore, can be comprehended only as "genus", as an internal, dumb generality which *naturally* unites the many individuals.

VII

Feuerbach, consequently, does not see that the "religious sentiment" is itself a social product, and that the abstract individual whom he analyses belongs to a particular form of society.

VIII

All social life is essentially *practical*. All mysteries which lead theory to mysticism find their rational solution in human practice and in the comprehension of this practice.

IX

The highest point reached by contemplative materialism, that is, materialism which does not comprehend sensuousness as practical activity, is the contemplation of single individuals and of civil society.

X

The standpoint of the old materialism is civil society; the standpoint of the new is human society, or social humanity.

XI

The philosophers have only *interpreted* the world, in various ways; the point is to *change* it.

KARL MARX

INTRODUCTION TO A CRITIQUE OF POLITICAL ECONOMY

I. PRODUCTION, CONSUMPTION, DISTRIBUTION, EXCHANGE (CIRCULATION)

1. *Production*

(*a*) To begin with, the question under discussion is *material production*. Individuals producing in a society, and hence the socially determined production of individuals, is of course the point of departure. The solitary and isolated hunter or fisherman, who serves Adam Smith and Ricardo as a starting point, is one of the unimaginative fantasies of eighteenth-century romances à *la* Robinson Crusoe; and despite the assertions of social historians, these by no means signify simply a reaction against over-refinement and reversion to a misconceived natural life. No more is Rousseau's *contrat social*, which by means of a contract establishes a relationship and connection between subjects that are by nature independent, at all based on this kind of naturalism. This is an illusion and nothing but the aesthetic illusion of the small and big Robinsonades. It is, on the contrary, the anticipation of "bourgeois society", which began to evolve in the sixteenth century and in the eighteenth century made giant strides towards maturity. The individual in this society of free competition seems to be rid of the natural ties etc. which made him an appurtenance of a particular, limited aggregation of human beings in previous historical epochs. The prophets of the eighteenth century, on whose shoulders Adam Smith and Ricardo were still wholly standing, envisaged this individual—a product of the dissolution of feudal society on the one hand and of the productive forces evolved since the sixteenth century on the other—as an ideal whose existence belongs to the past. They saw this individual not as an historical result, but as the starting-point of history; not as something evolving in the course of history, but posited by nature, because for them this individual was in conformity with nature, in keeping with their idea of human nature. This delusion has been characteristic of every new epoch hitherto. Steuart, who in some respects was in opposition to the eighteenth century and as an aristocrat tended rather to regard things from an historical standpoint, avoided this naïve view.

The farther back we trace the course of history, the more does the individual, and accordingly also the producing individual, appear to be dependent and to belong to a larger whole. At first, the individual in a still quite natural manner is part of the family and of the tribe which evolves from the family; later he is part of a community, of one of the different forms of the community which arise from the conflict and the merging of tribes. It is not until the eighteenth century that in the bourgeois society the various forms of the social texture confront the individual as merely means towards his private ends, as external necessity. But the epoch which produces this standpoint, namely that of the isolated individual, is precisely the epoch of the (as yet) most highly developed social (according to this standpoint, general) relations. Man is a ζωον πολιτικόν[1] in the most literal sense: he is not only a social animal, but an animal that can individualise himself only within society. Production by an isolated individual outside society— a rare event, which might occur when a civilised person who has already absorbed the dynamic social forces is accidentally cast into the wilderness—is just as preposterous as the development of speech without individuals who live *together* and talk to one another. It is unnecessary to dwell upon this point further. It need not have been mentioned at all, if this inanity, which had rhyme and reason in the works of eighteenth-century writers, were not expressly introduced once more into modern political economy by Bastiat, Carey, Proudhon, etc. It is of course very pleasant for Proudhon, for instance, to be able to explain the origin of an economic relationship—whose historical evolution he does not know—in an historico-philosophical manner by means of mythology; alleging that Adam or Prometheus hit upon the ready-made idea, which was then put into practice, etc. Nothing is more tedious and dull than the commonplace phantasies of *locus communis.*

Thus when we speak of production, we always have in mind production at a definite stage of social development, of production by individuals in a society. It might therefore seem that, in order to speak of production at all, we must either trace the various phases in the historical process of development, or else declare from the very beginning that we are examining *one* particular historical period, as for instance modern bourgeois production, which is indeed our real subject matter. All periods of production, however, have certain features in common; they have certain common categories. *Production*

[1] Zoon politikon—social animal.—*Ed.*

in general is an abstraction, but a sensible abstraction in so far as it actually emphasises and defines the common aspects and thus avoids repetition. Yet this *general* concept, or the common aspect which has been brought to light by comparison, is itself a multifarious compound comprising divergent categories. Some elements are found in all epochs, others are common to a few epochs. The most modern period and the most ancient period will have [certain] categories in common. Production without them is inconceivable. But although the most highly developed languages have laws and categories in common with the most primitive languages, it is precisely their divergence from these general and common features which constitutes their development. It is necessary to distinguish these definitions which apply to production in general, in order not to overlook the essential differences existing despite the unity that follows from the very fact that the subject, mankind, and the object, nature, are the same. For instance, on failure to perceive this fact depends the entire wisdom of modern economists who prove the eternity and harmony of existing social relations. For example, no production is possible without an instrument of production, even if this instrument is simply the hand. It is not possible without past, accumulated labour, even if this labour is only the skill acquired by repeated practice and concentrated in the hand of a savage. Capital is among other things also an instrument of production, and also past, materialised labour. Consequently capital is a universal and eternal relation given by nature—that is, provided one omits precisely those specific factors which turn the "instrument of production" or "accumulated labour" into capital. The whole history of the relations of production thus appears, for instance in Carey's writings, as a falsification malevolently brought about by the government.

Just as there is no production in general, so also there is no general production. Production is always a particular branch of production— e.g. agriculture, cattle-breeding, manufacture—or it is the *totality* of production. Political economy, however, is not technology. The relation of the general categories of production at a given social stage to the particular forms of production is to be set forth elsewhere (later).

Finally, not only is production particular production, but it is invariably only a definite social corpus, a social subject, that is engaged in a wider or narrower totality of production spheres. The relation of the academic presentation to the actual process does not belong here either. Production in general. Particular branches of production. Totality of production.

It is fashionable to preface economic works with a general part— and it is just this which appears under the heading "Production", see for instance John Stuart Mill—which deals with the general conditions of all production. This general part comprises or purports to comprise:

1. The conditions without which production cannot be carried on. This means in fact only that the essential factors required for any kind of production are indicated. But this amounts actually, as we shall see, to a few very simple definitions, which become reduced to trivial tautologies.

2. The conditions which promote production to a larger or smaller degree, as in the case of Adam Smith's progressive and stagnant state of society. To give this, which in Smith's work has its value as an *aperçu*, to give it scientific significance, research into the *degree of productivity* at various periods in the development of individual nations would have to be conducted; strictly speaking, such an investigation lies outside the framework of the subject, those aspects which are however relevant to it ought to be mentioned in connection with the development of competition, accumulation, etc. The answer in its general form amounts to the general statement that an industrial nation achieves its highest productivity when it is altogether at the height of its historical development. (In fact, a nation is at the height of its industrial development so long as, not the gain, but gaining remains its principal aim. In this respect the Yankees are superior to the English.) Or else that for example certain races, formations, climates, natural circumstances, such as maritime position, fertility of the soil, etc. are more conducive to production than others. This again amounts to the tautological statement that the production of wealth grows easier in the measure that its subjective and objective elements become available.

But all this is not really what the economists are concerned about in the general part. It is rather—see for example Mill—that production, as distinct from distribution etc., is to be presented as governed by eternal natural laws which are independent of history, and at the same time *bourgeois* relations are clandestinely passed off as irrefutable natural laws of society *in abstracto*. This is the more or less conscious purpose of the whole procedure. As regards distribution, however, it is said that men have indeed indulged in a certain amount of free choice. Quite apart from the crude separation of production and distribution and their real interconnection, it should be obvious from the outset that, however dissimilar the mode of distribution at the various stages of society may be, it must be possible, just as in the case of production, to emphasise the common aspects, and it must be likewise possible to confuse and efface all historical differences in laws that are *common to all mankind*. For example, the slave, the serf, the wage-worker, they all receive an amount of food enabling them to exist as a slave, serf or wage-worker. The conqueror who lives on tribute, or the official who lives on taxes, or the landowner who lives on rent, or the monk who lives on alms, or the clergyman who lives on tithes, all receive a portion of the social product which is determined by different laws from the portion of the slave, and so on. The two principal factors which all economists include in this section are: (1) property and (2) its protection by the judiciary, police, etc. Only a very brief reply is needed:

Regarding 1: production is always appropriation of nature by an individual within and with the help of a definite social organisation. In this context it is tautological to say that property (appropriation) is a condition of production. But it is quite ridiculous to make a leap from this to a distinct form of property, e.g. private property (this is moreover an antithetical form, which similarly presupposes *non-property* as a condition). History has shown, on the contrary, that common property (e.g. among the Indians, Slavs, ancient Celts, etc.) is the original form, and in the shape of communal property it plays a significant role for a long time. The question whether wealth develops faster under this or under that form of property is not yet under discussion at this point. It is tautological however to state that where no form of property exists there can be no production and hence no society either. Appropriation which appropriates nothing is a contradiction in terms.

Regarding 2. Safeguarding of what has been acquired, etc. If these trivialities are reduced to their real content, they say more than their authors realise, namely that each mode of production produces its specific legal relations, political forms, etc. It is a sign of crudity and lack of comprehension that organically coherent factors are brought into haphazard relation with one another, i.e. into a simple reflex connection. The bourgeois economists have merely in view that production proceeds more smoothly with modern police than, e.g., under club-law. They forget, however, that club-law too is law, and that the law of the stronger, only in a different form, still survives even in their "constitutional State".

While the social conditions appropriate to a particular stage of production are either still in the course of evolution or already in a state of dissolution, disturbances naturally occur in the process of production, although these may be of varying degree and extent.

To recapitulate: there are categories which are common to all stages of production and are established by reasoning as general categories; the so-called *general conditions* of all and any production, however, are nothing but abstract aspects which do not define any of the actual historical stages of production.

2. *The General Relations of Production to Distribution, Exchange and Consumption*

Before starting upon a further analysis of production it is necessary to consider the various sections which economists place alongside it.

The quite obvious conception is this: In the process of production members of society appropriate (produce, fashion) natural products in accordance with human requirements; distribution determines the share the individual receives of these products; exchange supplies him with the particular products into which he wants to convert the portion accruing to him as a result of distribution; finally, by consumption the products become objects of use, i.e. they are appropriated by individuals. Production creates articles corresponding to requirements; distribution allocates them according to social laws; exchange in its turn distributes the goods, which have already been allocated, in conformity with individual needs; finally, in consumption the product leaves this social movement, it becomes the direct object and servant of an individual need, which its use satisfies. Production thus appears as the point of departure, consumption as the goal, distribution and exchange as the middle, which has a dual form, since according to the definition, distribution is actuated by society and exchange is actuated by individuals. In production persons acquire an objective aspect, and in consumption objects acquire a subjective aspect; in distribution it is society which by means of dominant general rules mediates between production and consumption; in exchange this mediation occurs as a result of random decisions of individuals.

Distribution determines the proportion (the quantity) of the products accruing to the individual, exchange determines the products in which the individual claims to make up the share assigned to him by distribution.

Production, distribution, exchange and consumption thus form a proper syllogism; production represents the general, distribution and exchange the particular, and consumption the individual case which sums up the whole. This is indeed a sequence, but a very superficial one. Production is determined by general laws of nature; distribution by random social factors, it may therefore exert a more or less beneficial influence on production; exchange, a formal social movement, lies between these two; and consumption, as the concluding act, which is regarded not only as the final aim but as the ultimate purpose, falls properly outside the sphere of economy, except in so far as it in turn exerts a reciprocal action on the point of departure thus once again initiating the whole process.

The opponents of the economists who accuse the latter of crudely separating interconnected elements, either argue from the same standpoint or even from a lower one, no matter whether these opponents come from within or without the domain of political economy. Nothing is more common than the reproach that the economists regard production too much as a goal in itself, and that distribution is equally important. This argument is based on the concept of the economists that distribution is a separate and independent sphere alongside production. Another argument is that the different factors are not considered as a single whole; as though this separation had forced its way from the textbook into real life and not, on the contrary, from real life into the textbooks, and as though it were a question of the dialectical reconciliation of concepts and not of the resolution of actually existing conditions.

(a) Production and Consumption

Production is simultaneously consumption as well. It is consumption in a dual form—subjective and objective consumption. Firstly, the individual, who develops his abilities while producing, expends them as well, using them up in the act of production, just as in natural procreation vital energy is consumed. Secondly, it is consumption of the means of production, which are used and used up and in part (as for instance fuel) are broken down into simpler components. It similarly involves consumption of raw material which is absorbed and does not retain its original shape and quality. The act of production itself is thus in all its phases also an act of consumption. The economists concede this.

They call productive consumption, production that is simultaneously identical with consumption, and consumption which is directly concurrent with production. The identity of production and consumption amounts to Spinoza's proposition: *Determinatio est negatio*.

But this definition of productive consumption is only advanced in order to separate consumption that is identical with production from consumption in the proper sense, which is regarded by contrast as the destructive antithesis of production. Let us therefore consider consumption proper.

Consumption is simultaneously also production, just as in nature the production of a plant involves the consumption of elemental forces and chemical materials. It is obvious that man produces his own body, e.g. through feeding, one form of consumption. But the same applies to any other kind of consumption which in one way or another contributes to the production of some aspect of man. Hence this is consumptive production. Nevertheless, says political economy, this type of production that is identical with consumption is a secondary phase arising from the destruction of the first product. In the first type of production the producer assumes an objective aspect, in the second type the objects created by him assume a personal aspect. Hence this consuming production—although it represents a direct unity of production and consumption—is essentially different from production proper. The direct unity, in which production is concurrent with consumption and consumption with production, does not affect their simultaneous duality.

Production is thus at the same time consumption, and consumption is at the same time production. Each is simultaneously its opposite. But an intermediary movement takes place between the two at the same time. Production leads to consumption, for which it provides the material; consumption without production would have no object. But consumption also leads to production by providing for its products the subject for whom they are products. The product attains its final consummation in consumption. A railway on which no one travels, which is therefore not used up, not consumed, is potentially but not actually a railway. Without production there is no consumption, but without consumption there is no production either, since in that case production would be useless. Consumption produces production in two ways.

1. Because a product becomes a real product only through consumption. For example, a dress becomes really a dress only by being

worn, a house which is uninhabited is indeed not really a house, in other words a product as distinct from a simple natural object manifests itself as a product, becomes a product, only in consumption. It is only consumption which, by destroying the product, gives it the finishing touch, for the product is a product, not because it is materialised activity, but only in so far as it is an object for the active subject.

2. Because consumption creates the need for *new* production and therefore provides production with the conceptual, intrinsically actuating reason for production, which is the precondition for production. Consumption furnishes the impulse to produce, as well as providing the object which acts as the determining purpose of production. If it is evident that externally production supplies the object of consumption, it is equally evident that consumption *posits* the object of production as a *concept*, an internal image, a need, a motive, a purpose. Consumption furnishes the object of production in a form that is still subjective. There is no production without a need, but consumption re-creates the need.

This is matched on the side of production.

1. By the fact that production supplies the material, the object of consumption. Consumption without an object is no consumption, in this respect therefore, production creates, produces consumption.

2. But production provides not only the object of consumption, it also gives consumption a distinct form, a character, a finish. Just as consumption puts the finishing touch on the product as a product, so production puts the finishing touch to consumption. The object is not simply an object in general, but a particular object which must be consumed in a particular way, a way determined by production. Hunger is hunger; but the hunger that is satisfied by cooked meat eaten with knife and fork differs from hunger that devours raw meat with the help of hands, nails and teeth. Production thus produces not only the object of consumption but also the mode of consumption, no only objectively but also subjectively. Production therefore creates the consumer.

3. Production not only provides the material to satisfy a need, but it also provides the need for the material. When consumption emerges from its original primitive crudeness and immediacy—and its remaining in that state would be due to the fact that production was still primitively crude—then it is itself as a desire brought about by the object. The need felt for the object is induced by the perception of the

object. An *objet d'art* creates a public that has artistic taste and is able to enjoy beauty—and the same can be said of any other product. Production accordingly produces not only an object for the subject, but also a subject for the object.

Hence production produces consumption: 1. by providing the material of consumption; 2. by determining the mode of consumption; 3. by creating in the consumer a need for the objects which it first presents as products. It therefore produces the object of consumption, the mode of consumption and the urge to consume. Similarly, consumption produces the *predisposition* of the producer by positing him as a purposive requirement.

The identity of consumption and production has three aspects:

1. Direct identity: Production is consumption and consumption is production. Consumptive production and productive consumption. Economists call both productive consumption, but they still make a distinction. The former figures in their work as reproduction, the latter as productive consumption. All investigations concerning the former are concerned with productive and unproductive labour, concerning the latter with productive and non-productive consumption.

2. Each appears as a means of the other, as being induced by it; this is called their mutual dependence; they are thus brought into mutual relation and appear to be indispensable to each other, but nevertheless remain extrinsic to each other. Production provides the material which is the external object of consumption, consumption provides the need, i.e. the internal object, the purpose of production. There is no consumption without production, and no production without consumption. This proposition appears in various forms in political economy.

3. Production is not only simultaneously consumption, and consumption simultaneously production; nor is production only a means of consumption and consumption the purpose of production—i.e. each provides the other with its objects, production supplying the external object of consumption, and consumption the conceptual object of production—in other words, each of them is not only simultaneously the other, and not merely the cause of the other, but each of them by being carried through creates the other, it creates itself as the other. It is only consumption that consummates the process of production, since consumption completes the product as a product by destroying it, by consuming its independent concrete form.

Moreover, by its need for repetition consumption leads to the per-fection of abilities evolved during the first process of production and converts them into skills. Consumption is therefore the concluding act which turns not only the product into a product, but also the producer into a producer. Production, on the other hand, produces consumption by creating a definite mode of consumption, and by providing an incentive to consumption it thereby creates the capa-bility to consume as a requirement. The last kind of identity, which is defined in point 3, has been variously interpreted by economists when discussing the relation of demand and supply, of objects and needs, of needs created by society and natural needs.

After this, nothing is simpler for a Hegelian than to assume that production and consumption are identical. And this has been done not only by socialist *bellestrists* but also by prosaic economists, such as, Say, in declaring that if one considers a nation—or mankind *in abstracto* —then its production is its consumption. Storch has shown that this proposition of Say's is wrong, since a nation, for instance, does not consume its entire product, but must also provide means of production, fixed capital, etc. It is, moreover, wrong to consider society as a single individual, as in speculative reasoning. With an individual, production and consumption appear as different aspects of one act. The important point to be emphasised here is that if production and consumption be considered as activities of one individual or of separate individuals, they appear at any rate as aspects of one process in which production forms the actual starting-point and is, therefore, the predominating factor. Consumption, as a natural necessity, as a want, constitutes an internal factor of productive activity, but the latter is the starting-point of realisation and, therefore, its predominating factor, the act into which the entire process resolves itself in the end. The individual produces a certain article and turns again into himself by consuming it; but he returns as a productive and a self-reproducing individual. Consumption thus appears as a factor of production.

In society, however, the relation of the producer to his product, as soon as it is completed, is an outward one, and the return of the product to the individual depends on his relations to other individuals. He does not take immediate possession of it. Nor does the direct appropriation of the product constitute his purpose, when he produces in society. Between the producer and the product distribution steps in, which determines by social laws his share in the world of products; that is to say, distribution steps in between production and consumption.

Does distribution form an independent sector alongside and outside production?

(b) Production and Distribution

When looking through the ordinary run of economic works, one's attention is attracted forthwith by the fact that everything is mentioned twice, e.g. rent, wages, interest and profit figure under the heading distribution, while under the heading of production, land, labour and capital appear as factors of production. As to capital, it is evident from the outset that this is counted twice, first as a factor of production, and secondly as a source of income, i.e. as a determining and determinate form of distribution. Interest and profit appear therefore in production as well, since they are forms in which capital increases and grows, and are thus phases of its production. As forms of distribution, interest and capital presuppose capital as a factor of production. They are forms of distribution whose precondition is the existence of capital as a factor of production. They are likewise modes of reproduction of capital.

Wages represent also wage-labour, which is examined in a different section; the particular function that labour performs as a factor of production in the one case appears as a function of distribution in the other. If labour did not have the distinct form of wage-labour, then its share in the product would not appear as wages, as for instance in slavery. Finally rent—if we take the most advanced form of distribution by which landed property obtains a share in the products—presupposes large-scale landed property (strictly speaking, large-scale agriculture) as a factor of production, and not land in general; just as wages do not presuppose labour in general. The relations and modes of distribution are thus merely the reverse aspect of the factors of production. An individual whose participation in production takes the form of wage-labour will receive a share in the product, the result of production, in the form of wages. The structure of distribution is entirely determined by the structure of production. Distribution itself is a product of production, not only with regard to the content, for only the results of production can be distributed, but also with regard to the form, since the particular mode of men's participation in production determines the specific form of distribution, the form in which they share in distribution. It is altogether an illusion to speak of land in the section on production, and of rent in the section on distribution, etc.

Economists like Ricardo who are mainly accused of having paid exclusive attention to production, have accordingly regarded distribution as the exclusive subject of political economy, for they have instinctively treated the forms of distribution as the most precise expression in which factors of production manifest themselves in a given society.

To the single individual, distribution naturally appears as a social law, which determines his position within the framework of production, and within which he produces; distribution thus being antecedent to production. An individual who has neither capital nor landed property of his own is dependent on wage-labour from his birth as a consequence of social distribution. But this dependence is itself the result of the existence of capital and landed property as independent factors of production.

When one considers whole societies, still another aspect of distribution appears to be antecedent to production and to determine it, as though it were an ante-economic factor. A conquering nation may divide the land among the conquerors and in this way imposes a distinct mode of distribution and form of landed property, thus determining production. Or it may turn the population into slaves, thus making slave-labour the basis of production, or in the course of a revolution, a nation may divide large estates into plots, thus altering the character of production in consequence of the new distribution. Or legislation may perpetuate land ownership in certain families, or allocate labour as a hereditary privilege, thus consolidating it into a caste system. In all these cases, and they have all occurred in history, it seems that distribution is not regulated and determined by production but, on the contrary, production by distribution.

Distribution according to the most superficial interpretation is distribution of products; it is thus removed farther from production and made quasi-independent of it. But before distribution becomes distribution of products, it is (1) distribution of the means of production, and (2) (which is another aspect of the same situation) distribution of the members of society among the various types of production (the subsuming of the individuals under definite relations of production). It is evident that the distribution of products is merely a result of this distribution, which is comprised in the production process and determines the structure of production. To examine production divorced from this distribution which is a constituent part of it, is obviously idle abstraction; whereas conversely the distribution of products is automatically determined by that distribution which forms a primary factor of production. Ricardo, the economist of production *par excellence*, whose object was the understanding of modern production and of its distinct social structure, for this very reason declares that distribution, *not* production, is the proper subject of contemporary political economy. This is a witness to the banality of those economists who proclaim production as an eternal truth, and confine history to the domain of distribution.

The question as to the relation between that form of distribution that determines production and production itself, belongs obviously to the sphere of production. If it should be said that in this case at least, since production must proceed from a specific distribution of the means of production, distribution is to this extent antecedent to and a prerequisite of production, then the reply would be as follows. Production has indeed its conditions and prerequisites which are constituent elements of it. At the very outset these may have seemed to be naturally evolved. In the course of production, however, they are transformed from naturally evolved factors into historical ones, and although they may appear as natural preconditions for any one period, they are the historical result of another period. For example, the employment of machinery led to changes in the distribution of both the means of production and the product. Modern large-scale landed property has been brought about not only by modern trade and modern industry, but also by the application of the latter to agriculture.

The above-mentioned questions can be ultimately resolved into this: what role do general historical conditions play in production and the relations of production to the historical development as a whole? This question clearly belongs to the analysis and discussion of production.

In the trivial form, however, in which these questions have been raised above, they can be dealt with quite briefly. Conquests may lead to either of three results. The conquering nation may impose its own mode of production upon the conquered people (this was done, for example, by the English in Ireland during this century, and to some extent in India); or it may refrain from interfering in the old mode of production and be content with tribute (e.g. the Turks and Romans); or interaction may take place between the two giving rise to a new system as a synthesis (this occurred partly in the Germanic conquests). In any case it is the mode of production—whether that of the conquering nation or of the conquered or the new system brought about by a merging of the two—that determines the new mode of distribution employed. Although the latter appears to be a precondition of the new period of production, it is in its turn a result of production, a result not simply occasioned by the historical evolution of production in general, but by a specific historical form of production.

The Mongols, for example, who caused devastation in Russia, acted in accordance with their mode of production, cattle breeding, for which large uninhabited tracts are a fundamental requirement. The Germanic barbarians, whose traditional mode of production was agriculture with the aid of serfs and who lived scattered over the countryside, could the more easily adapt the Roman provinces to their requirements because the concentration of landed property carried out there had already uprooted the older agricultural relations. It is a long established view that over certain epochs people lived by plunder. But in order to be able to plunder, there must be something to be plundered, and this implies production. Moreover, the manner of plunder depends itself on the manner of production, e.g. a stock-jobbing nation cannot be robbed in the same way as a nation of cowherds.

The means of production may be robbed directly in the form of slaves. But in that case it is necessary that the structure of production in the country to which the slave is abducted admits of slave labour, or (as in South America, etc.) a mode of production appropriate to slave labour has to be evolved.

Laws may perpetuate a particular means of production, e.g. land, in certain families. These laws acquire economic significance only if large-scale landed property is in keeping with the social mode of production, as for instance in Britain. Agriculture was carried on in France on a small scale, despite the existence of large estates, which were therefore parcelled out by the Revolution. But is it possible, e.g. by law, to perpetuate the division of land into small lots? Landed property tends to become concentrated again despite these laws. The influence exercised by laws on the preservation of existing conditions of distribution, and the effect they thereby exert on production has to be examined separately.

(c) *Lastly, Exchange and Circulation*

Circulation is merely a particular phase of exchange or of exchange regarded in its totality.

Since exchange is simply an intermediate phase between production and distribution, which is determined by production, and consumption; since consumption is moreover itself an aspect of production, the latter obviously comprises also exchange as one of its aspects.

Firstly, it is evident that exchange of activities and skills, which takes place in production itself, is a direct and essential part of production. Secondly, the same applies to the exchange of products in so far as this exchange is a means to manufacture the finished product intended for immediate consumption. The action of exchange in this respect is comprised in the concept of production. Thirdly, what is known as exchange between dealer and dealer, both with respect to its organisation and as a productive activity, is entirely determined by production. Exchange appears to exist independently alongside production and detached from it only in the last stage, when the product is exchanged for immediate consumption. But (1) no exchange is possible without division of labour, whether this is naturally evolved or is already the result of an historical process; (2) private exchange presupposes private production; (3) the intensity of exchange, its extent and nature, are determined by the development and structure of production: e.g. exchange between town and country, exchange in the countryside, in the town, etc. All aspects of exchange to this extent appear either to be directly comprised in production or else determined by it.

The conclusion which follows from this is, not that production, distribution, exchange and consumption are identical, but that they are links or sections of a single whole, different aspects of one unit. Production is the decisive phase both with regard to the contradictory aspects of production and with regard to the other phases. The process always starts afresh with production. That exchange and consumption cannot be the decisive elements, is obvious, and the same applies to distribution in the sense of distribution of products. Distribution of the factors of production, on the other hand, is itself a phase of production. A distinct mode of production thus determines the specific mode of consumption, distribution, exchange and the *specific relations of these different phases to one another*. Production *in the narrow sense*, however, is in its turn also determined by the other aspects. For example, if the market, or the sphere of exchange, expands, then the volume of production grows and tends to become more differentiated. Production also changes in consequence to changes in distribution, e.g. concentration of capital, different distribution of the population in town and countryside, and the like. Production is, finally, determined by the demands of consumption. There is an interaction between the various aspects. Such interaction takes place in any organic entity.

3. The Method of Political Economy

When examining a given country from the standpoint of political economy, we begin with its population, the division of the population into classes, town and country, the sea, the different branches of production, export and import, annual production and consumption, prices, etc.

It would seem to be the proper thing to start with the real and concrete elements, with the actual preconditions, e.g. to start in the sphere of economy with population, which forms the basis and the subject of the whole social process of production. Closer consideration shows, however, that this is wrong. Population is an abstraction if, for instance, one disregards the classes of which it is composed. These classes in turn remain empty terms if one does not know the factors on which they depend, e.g. wage-labour, capital, and so on. These presuppose exchange, division of labour, prices, etc. For example, capital without wage-labour, without value, money, price, etc. is nothing. If one were to take population as the point of departure, it would be a very vague notion of a complex whole and through closer definition one would arrive analytically at increasingly simple concepts; from imaginary concrete terms one would move to more and more tenuous abstractions until one reached the most simple definitions. From there it would be necessary to make the journey again in the opposite direction until one arrived once more at the concept of population, which is this time not a vague notion of a whole, but a totality comprising many determinations and relations. The first course is the historical one taken by political economy at its inception. The seventeenth-century economists, for example, always took as their starting-point the living organism, the population, the nation, the state, several states, etc., but analysis led them always in the end to the discovery of a few decisive abstract, general relations, such as division of labour, money, and value. When these separate factors were more or less clearly deduced and established, economic systems were evolved which from simple concepts, such as labour, division of labour, demand, exchange value, advanced to categories like state, international exchange and world market. The latter is obviously the correct scientific method. The concrete concept is concrete because it is a synthesis of many definitions, thus representing the unity of diverse aspects. It appears therefore in reasoning as a summing up, a result, and not as the starting-point, although it is the real point of origin, and thus also the point of origin of perception and imagination. The first procedure attenuates meaningful images to abstract definitions, the second leads from abstract definitions by way of reasoning to the reproduction of the concrete situation. Hegel accordingly conceived the illusory idea that the real world is the result of thinking which causes its own synthesis, its own deepening and its own movement; whereas the method of advancing from the abstract to the concrete is simply the way in which thinking assimilates the concrete and reproduces it as a concrete mental category. This is, however, by no means the process of evolution of the concrete world itself. For example, the simplest economic category, e.g. exchange value, presupposes population, a population moreover which produces under definite conditions, as well as a distinct kind of family, or community, or state, etc. Exchange value cannot exist except as an abstract, *unilateral* relation of an already existing concrete organic whole. But exchange value as a category leads an antediluvian existence. Thus to consciousness—and this comprises philosophical consciousness—which regards the comprehending mind as the real man, and hence the comprehended world as such as the only real world; to consciousness, therefore, the evolution of categories appears as the actual process of production—which unfortunately is given an impulse from outside—whose result is the world; and this (which is however again a tautological expression) is true in so far as the concrete totality regarded as a conceptual mental totality, as a mental fact, is indeed a product of thinking, of comprehension; but it is by no means a product of the idea which evolves spontaneously and whose thinking proceeds outside and above perception and imagination, but is the result of the assimilation and transformation of perceptions and images into concepts. The totality as a conceptual entity seen by the intellect is a product of the thinking intellect which assimilates the world in the only way open to it, a way which differs from the artistic, religious and practically intelligent assimilation of this world. The concrete subject remains outside the intellect and independent of it—that is so long as the intellect adopts a purely speculative, purely theoretical attitude. The subject, society, must always be envisaged therefore as the precondition of comprehension even when the theoretical method is employed.

But have not these simple categories also an independent historical or natural existence preceding that of the more concrete ones? This depends. Hegel, for example, correctly takes ownership, the simplest legal relation of the subject, as the point of departure of the philosophy of law. No ownership exists, however, before the family or the relations of master and servant are evolved, and these are much more concrete relations. It would, on the other hand, be correct to say that families and entire tribes exist which have as yet only *possessions* and not *property*. The simpler category appears thus as a relation of simple family or tribal communities to property. In societies which have reached a higher stage the category appears as a comparatively simple relation existing in a more advanced community. The concrete substratum underlying the relation of ownership is however always presupposed. One can conceive an individual savage who has possessions; possession in this case, however, is not a legal relation. It is incorrect that in the course of historical development possession gave rise to the family. On the contrary, possession always presupposes this "more concrete category". One may, nevertheless, conclude that the simple categories represent relations or conditions which may reflect the immature concrete situation without as yet positing the more complex relation or condition which is conceptually expressed in the more concrete category; on the other hand, the same category may be retained as a subordinate relation in more developed concrete circumstances. Money may exist and has existed in historical time before capital, banks, wage-labour, etc. came into being. In this respect it can be said, therefore, that the simpler category expresses relations predominating in an immature entity or subordinate relations in a more advanced entity; relations which already existed historically before the entity had developed the aspects expressed in a more concrete category. The procedure of abstract reasoning which advances from the simplest to more complex concepts to that extent conforms to actual historical development.

It is true, on the other hand, that there are certain highly developed, but nevertheless historically immature, social formations which employ some of the most advanced economic forms, e.g. cooperation, developed division of labour, etc., without having developed any money at all, for instance, Peru. In Slavonic communities too, money —and its precondition exchange—is of little or no importance within the individual community, but is used on the borders where commerce with other communities takes place; and it is altogether wrong to assume that exchange within the community is an original constituent element. On the contrary, in the beginning exchange tends to arise in the intercourse of different communities with one another, rather than among members of the same community. Moreover, although money begins to play a considerable role very early and in diverse ways, it is known to have been a dominant factor in anitiquity only among nations developed in a particular direction, i.e. merchant nations. Even among the Greeks and Romans, the most advanced nations of antiquity, money reaches its full development, which is presupposed in modern bourgeois society, only in the period of their disintegration. The full potential of this quite simple category thus emerges historically not in the most advanced phases of society, and it certainly does not penetrate into all economic relations. For example, taxes in kind and deliveries in kind remained the basis of the Roman empire even at the height of its development; indeed a completely evolved monetary system existed in Rome only in the army, and it never permeated the whole complex of labour. Although the simpler category, therefore, may have existed historically before the more concrete category, its complete intensive and extensive development can nevertheless occur in a complex social formation, whereas the more concrete category may have been fully evolved in a more primitive social formation.

Labour seems to be a very simple category. The notion of labour in this universal form, as labour in general, is also extremely old. Nevertheless "labour" in this simplicity is economically considered just as modern a category as the relations which give rise to this simple abstraction. The Monetary System, for example, still regards wealth quite objectively as a thing existing independently in the shape of money. Compared with this standpoint, it was a substantial advance when the manufacturing or Mercantile system transferred the source of wealth from the object to the subjective activity—mercantile or industrial labour—but it still considered that only this circumscribed activity itself produced money. In contrast to this system, the Physiocrats assume that a specific form of labour—agriculture—creates wealth, and they see the object no longer in the guise of money, but as a product in general, as the universal result of labour. In accordance with the still circumscribed activity, the product remains a naturally developed product, an agricultural product, a product of the land *par excellence*.

It was an immense advance when Adam Smith rejected all restrictions with regard to the activity that produces wealth—for him it was labour as such, neither manufacturing, nor commercial, nor agricultural labour, but all of them. The abstract universality which creates wealth implies also the universality of the objects defined as wealth: they are products as such, or once more labour as such, but in this case past, materialised labour. How difficult and immense a transition this was is demonstrated by the fact that Adam Smith himself occasionally relapses once more into the Physiocratic system. It might seem that in this way merely an abstract expression was found for the simplest and most ancient relation in which human beings act as producers—irrespective of the type of society they live in. This is true in one respect, but not in another.

The fact that the specific kind of labour is irrelevant presupposes a highly developed complex of actually existing kinds of labour, none of which is any more the all-important one. The most general abstractions arise on the whole only when concrete development is most profuse, so that a specific quality is seen to be common to many phenomena, or common to all. Then it is no longer perceived solely in a particular form. This abstraction of labour is, on the other hand, by no means simply the conceptual resultant of a variety of existing concrete types of labour. The fact that the particular kind of labour employed is immaterial is appropriate to a form of society in which individuals easily pass from one type of labour to another, the particular type of labour being accidental to them and therefore irrelevant. Labour, not only as a category but in reality, has become a means to create wealth in general, and has ceased to be tied as an attribute to a particular individual. This state of affairs is most pronounced in the United States, the most modern form of bourgeois society. The abstract category "labour", "labour as such", labour *sans phrase*, the point of departure of modern economics, thus becomes a practical fact only there. The simplest abstraction, which plays a decisive rôle in modern political economy, an abstraction which expresses an ancient relation existing in all social formations, nevertheless appears to be actually true in this abstract form only as a category of the most modern society. It might be said that phenomena which are historical products in the United States—e.g. the irrelevance of the particular type of labour—appear to be among the Russians, for instance, naturally developed predispositions. But in the first place, there is an enormous difference between barbarians having a predisposition which makes it possible to employ them in various tasks, and civilised people who apply themselves to various tasks. As regards the Russians, moreover, their indifference to the particular kind of labour performed is in practice matched by their traditional habit of clinging fast to a very definite kind of labour from which they are extricated only by external influences.

The example of labour strikingly demonstrates how even the most abstract categories, despite their validity in all epochs—precisely because they are abstractions—are equally a product of historical conditions even in the specific form of abstractions, and they retain their full validity only for and within the framework of these conditions.

Bourgeois society is the most advanced and complex historical organisation of production. The categories which express its relations, and an understanding of its structure, therefore, provide an insight into the structure and the relations of production of all formerly existing social formations the ruins and component elements of which were used in the creation of bourgeois society. Some of these unassimilated remains are still carried on within bourgeois society, others however, which previously existed only in rudimentary form have been further developed and have attained their full significance, etc. The anatomy of man is a key to the anatomy of the ape. On the other hand, rudiments of more advanced forms in the lower species of animals can only be understood when the more advanced forms are already known. Bourgeois economy thus provides a key to the economy of antiquity, etc., but it is quite impossible [to gain this insight] in the manner of those economists who obliterate all historical differences and who see in all social phenomena only bourgeois phenomena. If one knows rent, it is possible to understand tribute, tithe, etc., but they do not have to be treated as identical.

Since bourgeois society is, moreover, only a contradictory form of development, it contains relations of earlier societies often merely in very stunted form or even in the form of travesties, e.g. communal ownership. Thus, although it is true that the categories of bourgeois economy are valid for all other social formations, this has to be taken *cum grano salis*, for they may contain them in an advanced, stunted, caricatured, etc. form, that is always with substantial differences. What is called historical evolution depends in general on the fact that the latest form regards earlier ones as stages in the development of itself and conceives them always in a one-sided manner, since only rarely and under quite special conditions is a society able to adopt a critical attitude towards itself; in this context we are not of course discussing historical periods which themselves believe that they are periods of decline. The Christian religion was able to contribute to an objective understanding of earlier mythologies only when its self-criticism was to a certain extent prepared, as it were potentially. Similarly, only when the self-criticism of bourgeois society had begun, was bourgeois political economy able to understand the feudal, ancient and oriental economies. In so far as bourgeois political economy did not simply identify itself with the past in a mythological manner, its criticism of earlier economies—especially of the feudal system against which it still had to wage a direct struggle—resembled the criticism that Christianity directed against heathenism, or which Protestantism directed against Catholicism.

Just as in general when examining any historical or social science, so also in the case of the development of economic categories is it always necessary to remember that the subject, in this context contemporary bourgeois society, is presupposed both in reality and in the mind, and that therefore categories express forms of existence and conditions of existence—and sometimes merely separate aspects—of this particular society, the subject; thus the category, *even from the scientific standpoint*, by no means begins at the moment when it is discussed *as such*. This has to be remembered because it provides important criteria for the arrangement of the material. For example, nothing seems more natural than to begin with rent, i.e. with landed property, since it is associated with the earth, the source of all production and all life, and with agriculture, the first form of production in all societies that have attained a measure of stability. But nothing would be more erroneous. There is in every social formation a particular branch of production which determines the position and importance of all the others, and the relations obtaining in this branch accordingly determine the relations of all other branches as well. It is as though light of a particular hue were cast upon everything, tingeing all other colours and modifying their specific features; or as if a special ether determined the specific gravity of everything found in it. Let us take as an example pastoral tribes. (Tribes living exclusively on hunting or fishing are beyond the boundary line from which real development begins.) A certain type of agricultural activity occurs among them and this determines land ownership. It is communal ownership and retains this form in a larger or smaller measure, according to the degree to which these people maintain their traditions, e.g. communal ownership among the Slavs. Among settled agricultural people—settled already to a large extent—where agriculture predominates as in the societies of antiquity and the feudal period, even manufacture, its structure and the forms of property corresponding thereto have, in some measure specifically agrarian features. Manufacture is either completely dependent on agriculture, as in the earlier Roman period, or as in the Middle Ages, it copies in the town and in its conditions the organisation of the countryside. Even in the Middle Ages capital—unless it was solely money capital—consisted of the traditional tools, etc. and retained a specifically agrarian character. The reverse takes place in bourgeois society. Agriculture to an increasing extent becomes just a branch of industry and is completely dominated by capital. The same applies to rent. In all forms in which landed property is the decisive factor, natural relations still predominate; in the forms in which the decisive factor is capital, social, historically evolved elements predominate. Rent cannot be understood without capital, but capital can be understood without rent. Capital is the economic power that dominates everything in bourgeois society. It must form both the point of departure and the conclusion and it has to be expounded before landed property. After analysing capital and landed property separately, their interconnection must be examined.

It would be inexpedient and wrong therefore to present the economic categories successively in the order in which they have played the dominant role in history. On the contrary their order of succession is determined by their mutual relation in modern bourgeois society and this is quite the reverse of what appears to be natural to them or in accordance with the sequence of historical development. The point at issue is not the role that various economic relations have played in the succession of various social formations appearing in the course of history; even less is it their sequence "as concepts" (Proudhon) (a nebulous notion of the historical process), but their position within modern bourgeois society.

It is precisely the predominance of agricultural peoples in the ancient world which caused the merchant nations—Phoenicians, Carthaginians—to develop in such purity (abstract precision) in the ancient world. For capital in the shape of merchant or money capital appears in that abstract form where capital has not yet become the dominant factor in society. Lombards and Jews occupied the same position with regard to mediaeval agrarian societies.

Another example of the various roles which the same categories have played at different stages of society are joint-stock companies, one of the most recent features of bourgeois society; but they arise also in its early period in the form of large privileged commercial companies with rights of monopoly.

The concept of national wealth finds its way into the works of the economists of the seventeenth century as the notion that wealth is created for the state, whose power, on the other hand, is proportional to this wealth—a notion which to some extent still survives even among eighteenth-century economists. This is still an unintentionally hypocritical manner in which wealth and the production of wealth are proclaimed to be the goal of modern states, and production itself is regarded simply as a means for producing wealth.

The disposition of material has evidently to be made in such a way that [section] one comprises general abstract definitions, which therefore appertain in some measure to all social formations, but in the sense set forth earlier. Two, the categories which constitute the internal structure of bourgeois society and on which the principal classes are based. Capital, wage labour, landed property and their relations to one another. Town and country. The three large social classes; exchange between them. Circulation. The (private) credit system. Three, the state as the epitome of bourgeois society. Analysis of its relations to itself. The "unproductive" classes. Taxes. National debt, public credit, Population, Colonies, Emigration. Four, international conditions of production. International division of labour. International exchange. Export and import. Rate of exchange. Five, world market and crises.

4. *Production*

Means of Production and Conditions of Production. Conditions of Production and Communication. Political forms and Forms of Cognition in Relation to the Conditions of Production and Communication. Legal Relations. Family Relations.

Notes regarding points which have to be mentioned in this context and should not be forgotten.

1. *War* develops [certain features] earlier than peace; the way in which as a result of war, and in the armies, etc. certain economic conditions, e.g. wage-labour, machinery, etc. were evolved earlier than within civil society. The relations between productive power and conditions of communication are likewise particularly obvious in the Army.

2. *The relation of the hitherto existing idealistic historiography to realistic historiography. In particular what is known as history of civilisation*, the old history of religion and states. (The various kinds of historiography hitherto existing could also be discussed in this context; the so-called objective, subjective (moral and others), philosophical [historiography].)

3. *Secondary and tertiary phenomena*, in general *derived* and *transmitted*, i.e. non-primary, conditions of production. The influence of international relations.

4. *Reproaches about the materialism of this conception; relation to naturalistic materialism.*

5. *Dialectics of the concepts productive power (means of production) and relations of production*, the limits of *this dialectical* connection, which does not abolish the real differences, have to be defined.

6. The unequal development of material production and, e.g. that of art. The concept of progress is on the whole not to be understood in the usual abstract form. Modern art, etc. This disproportion is not as important and difficult to grasp as within concrete social relations, e.g. in education. Relations of the United States to Europe. However, the really difficult point to be discussed here is how the relations of production as legal relations take part in this uneven development. For example the relation of Roman civil law (this applies in smaller measure to criminal and constitutional law) to modern production.

7. *This conception appears to be an inevitable development.* But vindication of chance. How? (Freedom, etc. as well.) (Influence of the means of communication. World history did not always exist; history as world history is a result.)

8. *The starting-point is of course the naturally determined factors;* both subjective and objective. Tribes, races, etc.

As regards art, it is well known that some of its peaks by no means correspond to the general development of society; nor do they therefore to the material substructure, the skeleton as it were of its organisation. For example, the Greeks compared with modern [nations], or else Shakespeare. It is even acknowledged that certain branches of art, e.g. the *epos*, can no longer be produced in their epoch-making classic form after artistic production as such has begun; in other words that certain important creations within the compass of art are only possible at an early stage in the development of art. If this is the case with regard to different branches of art within the sphere of art itself, it is not so remarkable that this should also be the case with regard to the entire sphere of art and its relation to the general development of society. The difficulty lies only in the general formulation of these contradictions. As soon as they are reduced to specific questions they are already explained.

Let us take, for example, the relation of Greek art, and that of Shakespeare, to the present time. We know that Greek mythology is not only the arsenal of Greek art, but also its basis. Is the conception of nature and of social relations which underlies Greek imagination and therefore Greek [art] possible when there are self-acting mules, railways, locomotives and electric telegraphs? What is a Vulcan compared with Roberts and Co., Jupiter compared with the lightning conductor, and Hermes compared with the *Crédit mobilier?* All mythology subdues, controls and fashions the forces of nature in the imagination and through imagination; it disappears therefore when real control over these forces is established. What becomes of Fama side by side with Printing House Square? Greek art presupposes Greek mythology, in other words that natural and social phenomena are already assimilated in an unintentionally artistic manner by the imagination of the people. This is the material of Greek art, not just any mythology, i.e. not every unconsciously artistic assimilation of nature (here the term comprises all physical phenomena, including society); Egyptian mythology could never become the basis of, or give rise to, Greek art. But at any rate [it presupposes] a mythology; on no account however a social development which precludes a mythological attitude towards nature, i.e. any attitude to nature which might give rise to myth; a society therefore demanding from the artist an imagination independent of mythology.

Regarded from another aspect: is Achilles possible when powder and shot have been invented? And is the Iliad possible at all when the printing press and even printing machines exist? Is it not inevitable that with the emergence of the press, the singing and the telling and the muse cease, that is the conditions necessary for epic poetry disappear?

The difficulty we are confronted with is not, however, that of understanding how Greek art and epic poetry are associated with certain forms of social development. The difficulty is that they still give us aesthetic pleasure and are in certain respects regarded as a standard and unattainable ideal.

An adult cannot become a child again, or he becomes childish. But does the naïveté of the child not give him pleasure, and does not he himself endeavour to reproduce the child's veracity on a higher level? Does not in every epoch the child represent the character of the period in its natural veracity? Why should not the historical childhood of humanity, where it attained its most beautiful form, exert an eternal charm because it is a stage that will never recur? There are rude children and precocious children. Many of the ancient peoples belong to this category. The Greeks were normal children. The charm their art has for us does not conflict with the immature stage of the society in which it originated. On the contrary its charm is a consequence of this and is inseparably linked with the fact that the immature social conditions which gave rise, and which alone could give rise, to this art cannot recur.

Written between the end of August and the middle of September 1857.

NAME AND AUTHORITY INDEX

SUBJECT INDEX